THE EVOLUTION
OF
URBAN SOCIETY

THE LEWIS HENRY MORGAN LECTURES/1965

presented at
The University of Rochester
Rochester, New York

THE EVOLUTION

OF

URBAN SOCIETY

EARLY MESOPOTAMIA AND PREHISPANIC MEXICO

BY ROBERT McC. ADAMS

ALDINE PUBLISHING COMPANY
CHICAGO

First published 1966 by
Aldine Publishing Company
529 South Wabash Avenue
Chicago, Illinois 60605

First paperback edition 1971

Sixth printing, 1973
ISBN 0-202-33016-8 (cloth); 0-202-33028-1 (paper)
Library of Congress Catalog Number 66-15195

Designed by David Miller
Printed in the United States of America

FOREWORD

LEWIS HENRY MORGAN WAS ASSOCIATED WITH THE UNIVERSITY OF Rochester from its founding. At his death he left it his manuscripts and library, and money to found a women's college. Save for a wing of the present Women's Residence Halls that is named for him, he remained without a memorial at the University until the Lewis Henry Morgan Lectures were begun.

These Lectures owe their existence to a happy combination of circumstances. In 1961 the Joseph R. and Joseph C. Wilson families made a gift to the University, to be used in part for the Social Sciences. Professor Bernard S. Cohn, at that time Chairman of the Department of Anthropology and Sociology, suggested that establishing the Lectures would constitute a fitting memorial to a great anthropologist and would be an appropriate use for part of this gift. He was supported and assisted by Dean (later Provost) McCrea Hazlett, Dean Arnold Ravin and Associate Dean R. J. Kaufmann. The details of the Lectures were worked out by Professor Cohn and the members of his Department.

The Morgan Lectures were planned initially as three annual series, for 1963, 1964 and 1965, to be continued if circumstances permitted. It was thought fitting at the outset to have each series focused on a particularly significant aspect of Morgan's work. Accordingly, Professor Meyer Fortes' 1963 Lectures were on kinship, Professor Fred Eggan devoted his attention to the American Indian, and Professor Robert M. Adams considered

v

the development of civilization. The first three series were inaugurated by Professor Leslie A. White, of the University of Michigan, who delivered two lectures on Morgan's life and work in January, 1963.

Publication of Professor Adams' Lectures makes them available to a wider public. A complete record of the informal daily seminars held during his visit at Rochester would fill additional volumes, were it available. Students and faculty alike recall these discussions with much pleasure.

The present volume is a revision of the third series, delivered by Professor Adams under the title, "Regularities in Urban Origins: A Comparative Study," on April 6-22, 1965.

ALFRED HARRIS
Department of Anthropology
The University of Rochester

PREFACE

THE SUBSTANCE OF THIS STUDY WAS PRESENTED IN APRIL, 1965, AS a third annual series of lectures at the University of Rochester in honor of Lewis Henry Morgan. I am indebted to a number of colleagues at Rochester, including especially Edward E. Calnek, Alfred Harris, and René Millon, for critical comments at the time they were delivered, which subsequently were incorporated in the revised text. Further suggestions and comments, which also have served as a basis for revision, were made by many of the participants at a Burg Wartenstein conference on "The Evolutionist Interpretation of Culture" in August, 1965. Particularly to be thanked for advice on that occasion are S. N. Eisenstadt, Friedrich Katz, and the conference chairman, Eric R. Wolf. Since other, less direct contributions to the final form of the manuscript must have stemmed from the plenary discussions of the conference, it is appropriate also to express my gratitude to the Wenner-Gren Foundation for Anthropological Research, under whose sponsorship this unusually fertile gathering of diverse specialists was convened. Among my colleagues at Chicago, I have benefited from comments made by Lloyd A. Fallers and Pedro Armillas. Finally, I am much indebted to Miguel Civil for a number of illuminating suggestions on how some of the Sumerological materials utilized in this study might be more solidly and imaginatively interpreted.

It was a singular pleasure to lecture on this theme in

L. H. Morgan's city and in his name. Surely we are all victims
to some degree of the narrowing professionalism and increasing timidity that accompanies the development of a mature
field, but anthropology still represents not so much an aca-
demic discipline in the prevailing sense as a broadly generalizing and comparative tradition of empirical inquiry. And one
of the most significant parts of that tradition began with Morgan, as did the recognition of the immediate subject of these
lectures as an enduring problem. However reoriented or di-
luted the line of descent at times may be, I hope that the main
course and conclusions of this study justifiably can be said to
continue in the direction he led us.

ROBERT McC. ADAMS

CONTENTS

LIST OF FIGURES

THE EVOLUTION
OF
URBAN SOCIETY

I

THE PROBLEM AND THE EVIDENCE

THE GENERALIZING, COMPARATIVE STUDY OF THE ORIGINS OF EARLY states has been an important research theme since before the emergence of anthropology as a conscious, distinctive intellectual approach. Indeed, the view that "savagery," "barbarism," and "civilization" form stages in a universal evolutionary sequence lay very close to the core of thought and speculation out of which anthropology arose. With the subsequent, increasingly conscious and refined, acquisition and analysis of both historical and ethnographic data, the deficiencies of this view became so strikingly apparent that for a long time the diversity of cultures received greater stress than their similarities. If today the tide has begun again to run in the opposite direction, perhaps at least a part of the explanation lies in the persuasiveness and vigor with which it has continued to be affirmed over the years that the early civilizations provide a significant example of broad regularities in human behavior.

This volume is concerned with the presentation and analysis of regularities in our two best-documented examples of early, independent urban societies. It seeks to provide as systematic a comparison as the data permits of institutional forms and trends of growth that are to be found in both of them. Emphasizing basic similarities in structure rather than the many acknowledged formal features by which each culture is rendered distinguishable from all others, it seeks to demonstrate that both the societies in question can usefully be regarded as variants of a single processual pattern.

1

The independent emergence of stratified, politically organized societies based upon a new and more complex division of
labor clearly is one of those great transformations which have
punctuated the human career only rarely, at long intervals. Obviously it deserves study as a crucial part of mankind's cumulative achievement. Yet surely it is also an untidy problem, on
whose component elements closure can be achieved only slowly
and painfully by marshalling every technique, every potential
source of insight and evidence in the arsenal of scholarship.
Herein, perhaps, lies the major reason for the durability and
attractiveness of the problem as a specifically anthropological
focus of interest.

The available evidence in the form of written sources, to
begin with, is too circumscribed in purpose and too limited
in amount to permit us to advance very far with the unaided
approach of the documentary historian. Hence we fall back
on other sources, which all too often are incommensurate with
whatever contemporary documentary data there may be. In
particular, archeology becomes a primary means of investigation, although the conclusions that archeological data permit
often seem to support an edifice of inferences different from
that erected on the basis of the documents. Still another line
of inquiry leads back through later materials of a literary or
mythical genre, relying on the attractive but always somewhat
hazardous assumption that usable accounts of preliterate events
and institutions have survived thus in traditional, encapsulated
form.

With sources as inconclusive as these, the only approach
that can retain even a vision of the central, crucial problem of
the emergence through time of a whole new set of institutional
relationships is one that is "contextual" rather than "textual"
in emphasis—that proceeds by offering, testing, and refining or
replacing as necessary a series of structured summaries or syn-
theses rather than confining analysis to fragmentary, isolated
cultural components. With some rare but notable exceptions,

on the whole it would appear that few but anthropologists combine a sense of the importance of the pivotal episodes of man's cultural evolution, a necessarily reconstructive or synthetic outlook, and a tolerance for ambiguity—all of which are required to work effectively on so elusive and yet intriguing a problem.

One other aspect of the origin of the earliest urbanized societies may be mentioned, which, arising from the character both of the data and of the transformation itself, has made it a special concern of scholarship within an anthropological tradition. Given the present limits to our detailed understanding of the process of change in any one area, we have a problem for which the comparative approach our discipline always has been identified with is highly suitable or perhaps even imperative. Given, further, the essentially independent internal sequences of cause and effect leading to statehood in widely different areas and epochs—whatever the precise role of external stimuli may have been—we have a problem that is peculiarly amenable to comparative treatment.

While the emergence of states has been a long-standing focus of anthropological discussion, it is impossible to deal more than very briefly here with the historical succession of views and issues that have characterized its development as a problem. The balanced appraisal of this development is a problem in intellectual history, a discipline with its own demanding methodology. A researcher in one generation, in attempting to trace the genealogy of the assumptions and concerns most vital to him, tends systematically to distort the issues that commanded the attention of his predecessors. Ideas, of course, are transmitted upward through time, from generation to generation, but they emerge and are periodically reinterpreted in a context of discussions and unspoken understandings that is continually changing and that is never confined to the bounds of a single discipline.

To cite an example pertinent to our own theme, what are

we to conclude from Lewis Henry Morgan's concluding insistence in *Ancient Society* on the transcendental role of a Supreme Intelligence in propelling along the evolution of civilization out of savagery and barbarism? To some, this insistence is part of a ringing refutation of the view that Morgan properly may be regarded as a progenitor of materialist conceptions, which he stimulated in others. To others, including myself, such an interpretation misconstrues both Morgan's major aims and his most enduring contributions.[1] But the more important point is that the issue of intellectual parentage, insofar as it rests on essentially post hoc evaluations, has as many answers as there are articulate, self-professed children. Only a quite different kind of study than we have yet seen, resting on all the technical apparatus of the competent intellectual historian with highly developed sensitivities to modes of thought and discourse of the Victorian era, may convincingly tell us how much of Morgan's deism was a formal concession to the temper of his times and how much a deeply held conviction that shaped his views of society.

In an even broader sense, the controversy over Morgan's formal relationship to (a variety of) idealistic and materialistic positions is irrelevant to the problems of cultural evolution as he understood them. These positions have assumed a detailed signficance—both stemming from and ramifying into spheres of political allegiance and action—unknown in Morgan's time. At least to judge from the variety of causal factors he adduced for successive evolutionary stages, Morgan's approach is better characterized by its flexibility than by any insistence on a philosophical position that is internally consistent by latter-day standards.

The problem of tracing the genealogy of evolutionary thinking with reference to the emergence of early states is further obscured by the changing context in which that thought

1. Cf. the exchange between M. E. Opler, T. G. Harding, and E. B. Leacock in *Cur. Anthrop.* 3 (1962), 478–79, and 5 (1964), 109–14.

has occurred. Since ancient history, ethnohistory, and archeology have essentially emerged as disciplines during the past century or so, the empirical base upon which reconstructions and theories have been formulated has been subject to radical and cumulative changes. In the later decades of the nineteenth century, Morgan and his colleagues knew little of the civilizations of the New World save an essentially synchronic picture that could be drawn from Spanish contact sources, and for the Old World had little to draw upon save the immediate antecedents of classical Greece and Rome and the testimony of the Old Testament. Within these limitations, the failure to perceive important developmental trends in late pre-Conquest nuclear American societies, for example, is hardly surprising. Even the reliance on extrapolations from putative "survivals," so often criticized now, may have been regarded at the time as an inadequate but inescapable and heuristically valid way in which to make a beginning with the data at hand. Of course, what contributed most to transforming this situation was the development of archeology to the point at which long, well-founded sequences of change and interrelationship in time and space could be formulated even in the absence of written records. But progress was almost equally marked in the recovery and decipherment of early documents.

In addition to the immense increase in the depth and breadth of available data over the past century or so, there have also been broad qualitative changes in the context of inquiry. Consider Morgan's classic formulation of the problem as he saw it:

As we re-ascend along the several lines of progress toward the primitive ages of mankind, and eliminate one after the other, in the order in which they appeared, inventions and discoveries on the one hand, and institutions on the other, we are enabled to perceive that the former stand to each other in progressive, and the latter in unfolding relations. While the former class have had a connection, more or less direct, the latter have been developed from a few primary germs of thought. Modern institutions plant their roots in the period of barbarism, into which their germs were transmitted from the previous period of savagery. They have had a lineal descent through the ages, with the streams of the blood, as well as a logical development.

Two independent lines of investigations thus invite our attention. The one leads through inventions and discoveries, and the other through primary institutions. With the knowledge gained therefrom, we may hope to indicate the principal stages of human development. [1963:4]

If my object were merely to insist anew on the authenticity of a viable scholarly tradition that descends to us from Morgan, it would be enough to perceive in this and similar passages an astonishingly modern emphasis on empirical exposition of the course of cultural evolution, a primary commitment, as Eleanor Leacock puts it, "to the rationality of historical law" (in Morgan 1963:vii). But the apparent anachronisms are as striking as this continuity of emphasis, and they shed a greater light on the changing context of study.

Morgan's tendency, in the first place, was to counterpose the cumulative growth of technology and related cultural items, on the one hand, with institutional developments that were visualized as the unfolding of potentialities already inherent in the germ. Thus he saw the idea of government, in a sense apparently not really distinguishable from the developed institutions of his own day, as having existed far back into the stage of savagery. What is missing, in our terms, is the world of thought succinctly summarized in Julian Steward's seminal expression, "levels of sociocultural complexity"—a framework of functionally interconnected institutions forming the structural core of a distinctive set of social systems.

Apparently not having known of the sharply discontinuous character of evolutionary advance generally, Morgan, in his conception of the course of cultural evolution, tended at times to assume that it had an "orthogenetic," preordained character. Moreover, rather than seeing the ordered sequence of small increments of change as a continuously adaptive process moving through time, he was content to chart the fortuitous presence of innovations in technique as convenient symbols of arbitrarily demarcated stages, without devoting much thought either to the character of the transitions between them or to the interplay of factors propelling the change. And, even where innovations of a societal rather than a technical character were brought forward, as in the case of the emphasis Morgan attached to the advent of private property, it is noteworthy that this was formulated not as the appearance of a new and profoundly important set of organized social relationships—a stratified grouping of classes—but only as a discrete new idea or feature.

In comparison with Morgan's usage, there has emerged not merely a difference in terminology but a significant conceptual advance beyond his demarcation in terms of convenient, easily recognizable traits of successive stages in what he seems to have regarded as a preordained path of progress leading upward to civilization. The more recent view is one that, instead, focuses attention on the disjunctive processes of transformation connecting one qualitatively distinctive level of sociocultural complexity with another. In fact, for purposes of systematically comparing the seemingly parallel and largely independent processes of growth leading to the formation of early urbanized polities or states, the concept of major, successive organizational levels now seems perhaps the single most indispensable one. Such levels may be regarded as broadly integrative patterns whose basic functional relationships tend to remain fixed (or, at least, tend to occur in fixed sequences), while their formal, superficial features vary widely from example to example. Given the much greater variability in the occurrence of individual features associated with the Urban Revolution than Morgan was aware of, including even such seemingly basic attributes as the degree of urbanism in settlement patterns and the invention of writing, the employment of the concept of levels permits us still to proceed beyond the acknowledgment of diversity to the recognition of genuine evolutionary parallelisms.

While the unearthing of new data on the history of cultural development undoubtedly played a part in changing the ways in which we formulate the course of cultural development, in the main the comparatively rapid, widespread, and unopposed acceptance of a view stressing the disjunctive aspects of evolutionary change probably is to be attributed to the broad shift toward similar views for biological evolution as a whole. After all, the stress that cultural evolutionists place on the expanded potentialities for adaptation conferred by new levels of cultural complexity surely has the Darwinian insistence on the central role of natural selection as its prototype. Just as ecological studies have become a major facet of research in modern biology, so we find a closely related growth in the emphasis given to studies in cultural ecology. Even the concept of levels of sociocultural integration itself is operationally very similar to the idea of organizational grades as the major units of evolutionary advance in the biological world. At a more abstract level, the main course of cultural evolution increasingly has come to be viewed as a succession of adaptive patterns, each new cultural type tending to spread and differentiate at the expense of less efficient precursors.

There is an interesting further parallelism between studies in evolutionary biology, on the one hand, and those in cultural evolution, on the other. Perhaps the most profound change in the former during recent decades has come through the recognition of the population as the unit within which adaptation takes place and upon which selective pressures act. The concept of a population as the unit of evolutionary potential, variable in the behavior of its constituents as well as in their genetic constitution, encourages the corresponding study of human societies rather than individuals as the adaptive units, even though corporate human behavior is mediated by the unique factor of culture. Perhaps also, although this remains more a matter of future possibility than of present performance, recognition of the importance of biological variability may encourage fuller study of cultural heterogeneity and dissonance as basic features of both adaptation and change.

There is no need to dwell at length on definitions of the entities with which this study deals. The major characteristics of early states have been repeatedly described, and in any case I am more concerned with the *process* of their growth than with a detailed discussion of their characteristics. There is no more adequate term evoking this process than that introduced by V. Gordon Childe, the "Urban Revolution."[2] Among its important advantages are that it places stress on the transformative character of the change, that it suggests at least relative rapidity, and that it specifies a restricted, urban locus within which the process was concentrated.

Yet it must be admitted that there are potential distortions involved in the use of the term as well as advantages, quite apart from the specific attributes Childe attaches to it. The more common usage of the word "revolution," for example, implies aspects of conscious struggle. Possibly there were overtones of consciousness about certain stages or aspects of the Urban Revolution, although the issue is unsettled. Any implication that such was generally the case, however, is certainly false. Again, the term perhaps implies a uniform emphasis on the growth of the city as the core of the process. At least as a form of settlement, however, urbanism seems to have been much less important to the emergence of the state, and even to the development of civilization in the broadest sense, than

2. Childe 1950. For a more substantive presentation of his views in the specific case of Mesopotamia see Childe 1952, esp. chap. 7. Both works emphasize archeological rather than textual findings, leading to a corresponding interpretive stress on technological aspects of change. No attempt has been made in this essay to duplicate or replace Childe's treatment of this theme.

social stratification and the institutionalization of political authority.

Still a further possible drawback is that uncritical use of the term may invoke an implicit, and therefore dangerous, assumption of the unity of all urban phenomena. This is at best a proposition that applies at so gross a level as to be hardly more than trivial, and yet it sometimes has served to divert attention toward misleading analogies with other cultural settings sharing only the fact of settlement in dense, "urban" clusters rather than toward the empirical investigation of the phenomena in hand. In short, the purpose of this study emphatically is not to generalize about the nature of cities but rather to discuss the processes by which, at least in some cases, they seem first to have come into existence. And as will become apparent, the achievement of these first steps in urban growth leads to a distinctive constellation of features that cannot be regarded simply as progressively approximating contemporary urbanism more and more closely.

In balance, the insights engendered by the term seem to outweigh its drawbacks. But the characteristics with which Childe sought to describe and associate it are less satisfactory. His criteria were the following: (1) increase in settlement size toward "urban" proportions; (2) centralized accumulation of capital resulting from the imposition of tribute or taxation; (3) monumental public works; (4) the invention of writing; (5) advances toward exact and predictive sciences; (6) the appearance and growth of long-distance trade in luxuries; (7) the emergence of a class-stratified society; (8) the freeing of a part of the population from subsistence tasks for full-time craft specialization; (9) the substitution of a politically organized society based on territorial principles, the state, for one based on kin ties; and (10) the appearance of naturalistic —or perhaps better, representational—art.

One objection to such a listing is that it gives us a mixed bag of characteristics. Some, like monumental architecture, can be unequivocally documented from archeological evidence but also are known to have been associated occasionally with non-civilized peoples. Others, like exact and predictive sciences, are largely matters of interpretation from evidence that is at best fragmentary and ambiguous. And still others, if not most of Childe's criteria, obviously must have emerged through a gradual, cumulative process not easily permitting distinctions in kind to be kept apart from those merely in degree. More-over, these characteristics differ radically from one another in their importance as causes, or even as indices, of the Urban Revolution as a whole. The significance of the reappearance of representational art—indeed, its initial appearance, insofar as it deals with the human figure—for example, is at least not immediately apparent.

A more basic objection to any such listing is that its eclec-ticism embraces fundamental contradictions as to purpose. Childe echoes Morgan in seeking to identify the Urban Revo-lution by a series of traits whose vestiges the specialist can conveniently recognize. This was a reasonable procedure for Morgan's purpose, the initial delineation of a succession of stages, but with Childe, on the other hand, we enter an era in which the emphasis shifted toward providing accounts with explanatory power as well.

The term "Urban Revolution" implies a focus on ordered, systematic *processes* of change through time. Hence the identi-fying characteristics of the Urban Revolution need to be more than loosely associated features (no matter how conveniently recognizable), whose functional role is merely assumed and which are defined in terms of simple presence or absence. Usefully to speak of an Urban Revolution, we must describe a functionally related core of institutions as they interacted and evolved through time. From this viewpoint, the characteristics Childe adduces can be divided into a group of primary vari-ables, on the one hand, and a larger group of secondary, de-pendent variables, on the other. And it clearly was Childe's

view that the primary motivating forces for the transformation
lay in the rise of new technological and subsistence patterns.
The accumulative growth of technology and the increasing
availability of food surpluses as deployable capital, he argued,
were the central causative agencies underlying the Urban
Revolution.

This study is somewhat differently oriented; it tends to
stress "societal" variables rather than "cultural" ones. Perhaps
in part, such an approach is merely an outgrowth of limitations
of space; social institutions lend themselves more easily to the
construction of a brief paradigm than do the tool types or pottery styles with which the archeologist traditionally works. But
I also believe that the available evidence supports the conclusion that the transformation at the core of the Urban Revolution lay in the realm of social organization. And, while the
onset of the transformation obviously cannot be understood
apart from its cultural and ecological context, it seems to have
been primarily changes in social institutions that precipitated
changes in technology, subsistence, and other aspects of the
wider cultural realm, such as religion, rather than vice versa.

Perhaps it is for this reason that I shall largely avoid the
word "civilization" in this discussion. It refers inclusively to
the totality of an expansive and long-lived cultural manifesta-
tion, and hence reduces the possibility of erecting meaningful
paradigmatic models—"cores"—for purposes of comparison.
Consider the use of the word by A. L. Kroeber, its most distinguished exponent:

To the historian, civilizations are large, somewhat vague segments of the totality of historical events which it may sometimes be
convenient or useful to segregate off from the remainder of history, and which tend to evince certain dubiously definable qualities
when so segregated. To the student of culture, civilizations are
segments of the totality of human history when this is viewed less
for its events, and less as behavior and acts, than as the more enduring products, forms, and influences of the actions of human
societies. To the student of culture, civilizations are segregated or

delimited from one another by no single criterion: partly by geography, partly by period; partly by speech, religion, government, less by technology; most of all, probably, by those activities of civilization that are especially concerned with values and the manifest qualities of style. [1953:275].

To be sure, Kroeber goes on to observe that "the form and structure possessed by civilizations invite a comparative morphology." But, in practice, the forms upon which he concentrates are indefinitely inclusive and distinctive for each civilization, as reflected in the fact that they find their most succinct expression in stylistic terms rather than in analytical terms that are potentially expressive of genuine regularities.

This is not to deny that the term "civilization" has advantages for other purposes, and in particular for characterizing state societies as they are distinguished from societies of lesser degrees of complexity. As Morgan already saw, civilizations are associated with qualitatively greater scale and internal differentiation than other societies or cultures, and it is entirely proper to set them aside as a class under this term even if the terms for his other equally inclusive categories, "savagery" and "barbarism," will seem to most anthropologists excessively ethnocentric and pejorative.

The cultural referent of the term "civilization" confers still other advantages when the objective is not processual explanation of growth but the synchronic analysis of a wide range of potentially interacting variables. A distinction between great and little civilizational traditions as posited by Robert Redfield (1953), for example, encourages us to look for creative patterns of interaction between different social constituencies—on the one hand, the conscious, literate (generally), syncretistic, philosophical, mythopoeic expression of the urbanized elite and, on the other, the little traditions of the rural peasantry, more limited in scope, more variable in both space and time. But, without denying that important insights may flow from this line of analysis, I would only insist that it has little to do with an attempt to account for the *genesis* of civilized society. Like the idea of a folk-urban continuum, which Redfield also posited, its value is more heuristic than truly explanatory.

The term "state" on the other hand, is useful for this discussion in that it centers on the political order, one of our major subjects of inquiry. For all the acrimonious debate about the essential features of state societies, they may reasonably be defined as hierarchically organized on political and territorial lines rather than on kinship or other ascriptive groups and relationships. Internally, at least, even primitive states tended to monopolize the use of force for the preservation of order, while externally they exercised a degree of sovereignty. Like the state itself, these root characteristics emerged at varying rates during the course of the Urban Revolution. While our recognition of them is often rendered dubious and never precise by the nature of the data, they clearly serve to distinguish a new, qualitatively more complex and extensive, mode of social integration.

References made earlier to the "core" of the Urban Revolution as a changing, functionally related group of social institutions prompt a comparison of this usage with that of Julian Steward, from whom I have borrowed the term in slightly altered form. For Steward, the "core" of a culture is a nexus of basic institutions and relationships, a statement of the "functional interdependency of features in a structural relationship" (1955:94). The recognition of culture "cores" as distinct from "secondary" features provides the basis for a typology of cultures stressing their most essential, invariant characteristics and, hence, for a study of processual regularities common to the appearance of a given cultural type. That far I would agree fully with him. However, while he concedes that social, political, and even religious patterns may be empirically determined to fall within the limits of the core as an operational concept, for him the concept centers on "the constellation of features which are most closely related to subsistence activities and economic arrangements" (p. 37). Here, at least with respect to his emphasis upon ecological adaptation as the primary source of change—"the extracultural factor in the fruitless assumption that culture comes from culture" (p. 36)—and upon the separation of economic forms of behavior from the social and political institutions that generally mediated them, it seems necessary to part company with him.

Steward himself concedes that "the simpler cultures are more directly conditioned by their environment than advanced ones" (p. 40), so at least for the latter we are entitled to doubt whether his view is correct that the only (or even the major) effective locus of change is to be found outside culture rather than within it. The effect of regarding ecological response as the primary creative process, it may be pointed out, is to encourage the search for misleadingly self-generating extracultural factors, such as population pressure or the managerial requirements of irrigation systems, as the effectively independent causes of cultural development. Particularly in these two instances, the evidence for the period of the emergence of the early states strongly suggests that they were neither independent causal agencies "outside" culture nor of sufficient overall importance even to be viewed as among the major, closely interacting factors precipitating cultural change.

No matter how defined, the distinction between a cultural core and secondary features is one that is operationally imposed on, not inductively derived from, the empirical data of history and archeology. It is applied a posteriori as an explanatory tool, both to focus attention on certain apparently strategic aspects of change and to elucidate a plausible cause-and-effect sequence. It involves discrimination as to the significant aspects of reality—significance in this case being associated with the achievement of the major features that we associate with the Urban Revolution. As such, it concentrates on the cluster of institutions whose development characterizes the full achievement of the Urban Revolution. It emphasizes those features which exhibit a rapid, qualitative advance rather than those which change more slowly or which, in spite of internal changes, maintain a relatively high degree of continuity as to both form and function. In a word, any meaningful use of the concept of a culture core in the study of change involves special stress on *emergent* phenomena. But, at least, any explanatory, causal orientation to the study of history—and ultimately there is no other that justifies the effort—involves a precisely similar process of selection of what constitute the significant trends, institutions, and events from the point of view of understanding change.

There are also dangers of teleology in the employment of the concept of a culture core as an analytic device. Almost certainly the core trends we associate with the Urban Revolution —social stratification, urbanization, political differentiation, militarization, craft specialization, and the like—were subject repeatedly to brakings and reversals along the way, even though we generally remain ignorant of these irregularities and can perceive only the cumulative transformation that the Urban Revolution brought about. But, just as evolutionary biologists have done, we must continue to speak of trends for as long as our evidence points to them, while recognizing that change is a *continuously* adaptive process in which the ends are never immanent.

The concept of a culture core implies the less obvious, and hence perhaps more dangerous, connotations of interdependency and compactness. These connotations may create no distortions for earlier, simpler stages of cultural development, to which the fully integrated, seamless web of classical functionalism applies as a reasonably close approximation of reality. But, in the case of complex state societies, their rise is accompanied by the progressive dissociation of major institutional spheres from one another, the differentiation of what S. N. Eisenstadt (1964: 376) describes as "relatively specific and autonomous symbolic and organizational frameworks within the confines of the same institutionalized system." Hence the functionalist model may become progressively less relevant as the Urban Revolution proceeds. To take our specific case, the employment of the concept of a culture core should not be taken to imply that social stratification and the growth of autonomous political organs proceeded in continuous, intimate interdependency throughout the period of the Urban Revolution and beyond. At least at times, they seem to have been, as Eisenstadt (1963: 93) insists, "two analytically distinct and independent variables."

A basic question relating to the possibility of discontinuities in the causally interrelated web of changes that constitutes the Urban Revolution concerns the rate and duration of the transformation itself. To the degree that we visualize it as really abrupt or rapid—rapid in absolute terms and not merely in relation to the long antecedent period of sedentary village farming, which was characterized at most by few and limited structural changes—to that degree, the possibility that it had internally distinctive subphases or changes of direction assumes less importance. To that degree also, the process as a whole can be regarded as an abrupt "step" upward to new levels of sociocultural complexity, in contrast with the "ramp" that is implied if the process continued over many generations or even centuries.

These terms "step" and "ramp" were recently introduced by Robert J. Braidwood and Gordon R. Willey (1962:351) especially to characterize an apparent difference between the course of development in Mesopotamia and Mesoamerica, respectively. The metaphor of the ramp introduces a source of potential teleological distortion, for it suggests a smooth upward progression, a uniformly unfolding series of trends whose common direction was somehow fixed from the outset. The step metaphor, on the other hand, tends to compress all aspects of the Urban Revolution into the same brief, inexplicably creative period. Since our knowledge becomes progressively fuller with the later phases of the archeological and historical sequences leading to all the early states, a corollary of the step metaphor is the assumption that we can infer all the essential part of the transformation at the earliest point in the archeological record at which there is any evidence of rapidly increasing differentiation or complexity. It would follow, to continue with the step metaphor, that most or all of the crucial directions of change somehow were fixed inconveniently far back in prehistory and that our written and ethnohistorical records can tell us only about minor cyclical fluctuations superimposed on sociocultural systems that were already fully stabilized.

My own bias is to rely, insofar as possible, on the ramp metaphor, at least for purposes of this discussion. The advantages of doing so are primarily heuristic. First, it forces us to come to grips with the Urban Revolution as an intelligible sequence of change rather than simply accepting it as an almost mystically sudden impulse. Second, the ramp metaphor brings at least the later phases of the transformation in both the Old and the New World down into the range of the rich source of questions and insights available only in written documents. Recognizing that the future tide of discoveries may compel us to abandon all the documentary sources as primary, contemporary accounts of the initial Urban Revolution and, hence, to fall back on the step metaphor and consequently on archeological evidence alone, to do so as an a priori position seems self-defeating.

Just as we may isolate for analytical purposes a strategic institutional locus of change, a culture core, and a temporal locus during which fundamental changes proceeded at least relatively rapidly, the Urban Revolution, so we must specify a geographical locus. It has already been noted that the term "Urban Revolution" focuses our attention on the city as both the consequence and the chief locus of the Urban Revolution. But, of course, the formation of a city can be understood only in relation to its hinterland, in spite of how seemingly resistant to change the peasantry in that hinterland sometimes may be. Moreover, both the individual early city and its hinterland rarely if ever must have occurred except as parts of an interacting network composed of many such entities. Particularly appropriate for the description of such networks is the recently introduced concept of a key area and its surrounding symbiotic region (Palerm and Wolf 1957:29; Sanders 1956:115). As the use of this concept to understand the cultural primacy of areas like the Valley of Mexico over long periods implies, key areas must be considered not in isolation but in close interaction with their often highly variable surroundings. While obvious in principle, in practice this point often tends to be overlooked. There is a perhaps unavoidable tendency, for example, for archeologists to become preoccupied with the major centers in which monumental construction and creative activity were concentrated at the expense of depressed, dependent outlying settlements whose specialized resources and "surpluses" may have been indispensable for the former. Or, again, there are pitfalls that are not often recognized in regarding urban states as based on agriculture, and agriculture as implying an exclusively sedentary way of life. On this basis, the symbiotic region within which early states arose might be defined too narrowly in terms of the limits of sedentary agriculture. But, in so doing, at least in some cases we would ignore what may have been vital, causal elements in the Urban Revolution. It will be argued presently that, at least in Mesopotamia, nomadism was one of the strategic disequilibrating factors that may have set the core processes of the Urban Revolution into motion and, further, that the earliest durable patterns of political organization to extend beyond the confines of the individual city-state received their impetus from semitribalized entities whose recent nomadic background can be assumed.

I propose to contrast and compare only two from among the considerable number of examples of the Urban Revolution for which evidence might be adduced. In part, the choice

of Mesopotamia and central Mexico reflects the special limitations of my own knowledge. But, to a degree at least, the
opposite is also true, for my own specialized interest in the
two areas developed with, not before, my preoccupation with
the growth and functioning of patrimonial societies and primitive states as a theoretical problem. Hence it may be useful
more fully to develop the arguments in favor of selecting
these two examples.

To begin with, the advantages of selecting an Old World
and a New World example of early states as the major bases
for comparison seem plain. By doing so we tend to minimize
the possibility that similarities reflect genetic interconnection,
that is, the operation of cultural diffusion, rather than independently occurring (and therefore presumably "lawful,"
cause-and-effect) regularities. For all Old World civilizations
save that in Mesopotamia, it is at least a matter of continuing
debate whether the course of development may not have been
significantly influenced by a neighboring *civilizational* nucleus
of earlier date. This problem is by no means entirely elimi-
nated by including a New World example as well as an Old
World one, as currently intensifying interest in the possibilities
of early trans-Pacific interconnections shows, but it is at least
held to a minimum.

Julian Steward, to be sure, has rightly insisted that even
a considerable degree of diffusion may not seriously distort the
regularities of change. Decrying the tendency to treat diffusion
as "a mechanical and unintelligible, though universal, cause,"
he believes that "one may fairly ask whether each time a society
accepts diffused culture, it is not an independent recurrence of
cause and effect" (1955:182). But, at any rate, the problem of
how extensive the external factors in the formation of a primitive state must have been before having a significant effect on
its basic course and patterns of development is a problem for
empirical study rather than a priori theorizing. Therefore it
surely is desirable to base systematic comparisons primarily on

a selection of the most divergent and nearly independent of the existing examples.

In a recent paper Morton Fried has proposed the distinction between "pristine" and "secondary" states, arguing that the latter followed a distinctive course of development based on the superimposition of a conqueror stratum over the bulk of the local population, while the former "developed *sui generis* out of purely local conditions" (1960:729). I tend to agree with his decision to group all the major civilizational nuclei (Mesopotamia, Egypt, Indus Valley, North China, Mesoamerica, and Peru) as "pristine" examples, in contrast to all other possible cases. But the important point is that Fried acknowledges the validity of the distinction between voluntary states and externally imposed or inspired ones, so that the question of whether all the Old World examples belong in this category must again be an empirical one. And, since our primary interest is with the "pristine" case (or, we may hope, cases), again it seems best to work with but a single example from within the Old World *oikoumene* and to contrast it with one from the New World.

In the Old World, Mesopotamia offers certain obvious advantages quite apart from its apparent temporal priority; or, perhaps, if we phrase the matter more honestly, it offers relatively fewer and less serious disadvantages. At least in contrast with Egypt, the Indus Valley, and China, a more ample, diversified, and continuous archeological record is available of the antecedent stages leading up to the achievement of an "urban" level of sociocultural complexity. In Egypt, to be sure, Sir Flinders Petrie's sequence dating scheme, although derived exclusively from seriation studies, has stood the test of time and corroborative radiocarbon-dating analyses as reflecting continuity of occurrence. But exposures continue to be limited very largely to graves, and a processual understanding of changing patterns of social organization will never be obtained from the mortuary cult alone. Precivilizational levels of settlements in the alluvial plain of the Indus still remain as poorly known as those in the Nile Valley; and developments leading to that civilization are not likely to be well represented in excavations of small-scale village settlements of marginal hill-folk in neighboring Baluchistan. For China, later still and hence exposed for a still longer time to a variety of direct and indirect influences from civilization farther west, the problem of the incompleteness of the archeological record during the course of the Urban Revolution is equally acute.

There are further valid reasons for the selection of Mesopotamia if we consider the evidence available just after each nuclear area had crossed the threshold of "urban" complexity. In spite of the many problems involved in interpreting the early Sumerian cuneiform texts, at any rate a considerable degree of understanding is possible for the greater number that fall into non-"literary" categories. Further, the archeological sequence has been worked out with considerable precision and can be linked not only with the usual succession of temples but also with palaces, city walls, private houses, tombs, and "royal" graves, and even with individuals whose names appear as kings in reliable later records of the dynastic succession. By contrast, our information on Egypt continues to come virtually entirely from tombs.

With respect to a few aspects of social organization—for example, careers of individual rulers, nobles, and members of the administrative elite—Egyptian mortuary practices inform us much more fully than do their Mesopotamian counterparts. But, in general, and particularly with respect to quantitative aspects of economic behavior for which both the mass of Mesopotamian texts and the relatively wide extent of Early Dynastic Mesopotamian excavations in settlement debris are pertinent, nothing is possible in Egypt that approaches the breadth and depth of reconstruction of functioning Mesopotamian political, social, and economic institutions that the cuneiform texts make possible.

For the Indus Valley, the problem is not one of the scale of archeological exposure but of the relatively poor stratigraphic, and hence chronological, control that was characteristic of most of the early, large-scale work there. Furthermore, only a very limited body of inscriptional materials is yet available, and it is still untranslated. Only China remains as an instance of civilizational development that is comparable to Mesopotamia in quantity and quality of the available evidence. In that case, its relatively late development increases the likelihood that it may be "secondary" rather than "pristine" in significant ways and also increases the possibility that any observed similarities with the prehispanic civilizations of the New World may reflect cultural influences rather than evolutionary parallelisms.

For the New World, the case is more simply stated. Archeological work in Mesoamerica has been much more extensive and has continued for longer, with earlier attention to secure stratigraphic control, a geographically wider and much fuller knowledge of regional developmental sequences than in the central Andean area. A large and important body of Spanish ethnohistorical material is available on both these areas, but only from Mesoamerica are a number of prehispanic written documents also available.

An additional drawback to the Andean area is that archeological knowledge is much fuller from coastal areas, which were overwhelmed, destroyed as independent political entities, and partly depopulated during the final generations of Inca expansionism before the Spanish Conquest. As a result, the body of Spanish ethnohistorical material for those areas is extremely limited. On the other hand, the antecedents of the Inca Empire in the highlands, in the area where the Inca had their origins and where Spanish descriptions of the floruit of their empire are more adequate, still remain only fitfully illuminated by small-scale excavations that are widely scattered in space and time. In short, the utility of the already limited data is further reduced by the fact that the area whose prehistoric sequence is best known archeologically differs ecologically and culturally from the area where the imperial organization that is described in the ethnographical sources first arose and became characteristic.

Thus a persuasive case can be made, based on the extent and type of the available evidence, for concentrating upon Mesoamerica in outlining comparisons with the course of the Urban Revolution in the Old World. Within Mesoamerica, however, a further narrowing of geographical focus is indicated by striking differences in ecological potential and cultural tradition from region to region. Maya civilization, centered in the lowland rain forests of Guatemala, is virtually as distinctive and autonomous in relation to Mesoamerican civilization as a totality as Egyptian civilization is within the general rubric of early Near Eastern civilization. Only the development of the study of Mesoamerica within the bounds of a unified and intercommunicating anthropological discipline, in contrast to the growth in the Old World of entirely separate philological specializations, has obscured this similarity in geographic and cultural scale between Mesoamerica and the Near East as a whole.

For the special purposes of a comparative study the Maya area is not an especially suitable one. The disruption and termination of many of its major cultural patterns at about the end of the Classic period (ca. 900 A.D.), and the undeniable Mexican influence on later phases of development that continued only in previously marginal regions like northern Yucatán, create special problems that seriously deter a consideration of possible parallelisms.

The most useful unit equivalent to southern Mesopotamia as a civilizational nucleus is central Mexico. Although in large part a rugged highland region that is strikingly different from the alluvial plains adjoining the lower Tigris and Euphrates Rivers, the two regions are closely comparable in terms of population potential, degree of political centralization and urbanization. Moreover, while continuous, uninterrupted patterns of settlement do not seem to have been characteristic of central

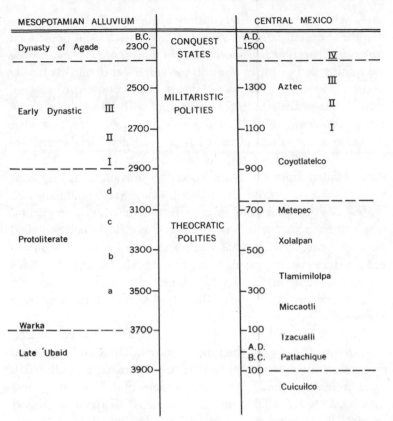

FIGURE 1. Comparative chronologies for early Mesopotamia
and prehispanic central Mexico

Mexico, at least the region as a whole provides a relatively continuous sequence when a succession of different religious and
political centers are taken into account. Having constituted the
core of the Aztec realm at the time of the arrival of the Spaniards, it furnishes us also with that special wealth of recorded
observational detail which the Spaniards accorded to their principal Mesoamerican adversaries.

A chronological framework for the comparison of Mesopo-

tamia with central Mexico is outlined in Figure 1. Having specified these examples of the rise of early states as the ones upon
which it seems best to concentrate, we must consider more fully
the quality and quantity of available empirical data. It is hardly
necessary to discuss the potentialities and limitations of archeological data in abstract terms for dealing with historical or socio-
logical problems; surely they are now commonplaces. But what
are some of the effects of the changing character of documentation, both at different time periods and as the Old World is
differentiated from the New, upon the prevailing assumptions
and emphases of study? Before contrasting Mesopotamian with
central Mexican societies in an effort to elicit developmental
regularities, a problem must be introduced to which we shall
return repeatedly: To what degree may the observed similarities or differences between these two widely separated regions
possibly be only artifacts of accidental differences in the data
or in the dominant directions that studies in each of them have
followed?

One set of conditions applies to the Early Village horizon
in both areas, that is, to the time of consolidation and expansion
of a sedentary, agricultural way of life organized around small-
scale, relatively undifferentiated settlements. First and most
important, the available material for that horizon is almost
exclusively archeological. Particularly in Mesopotamia, most
exposures are limited to deep pits in massive later sites, limiting
the scale of excavations and often preventing the recovery of
complete building plans. An increasingly serious problem in
both areas is the disproportionately greater share of attention
that the earliest agricultural origins are receiving than subsequent phases in the consolidation of a sedentary way of life.
Late prehistoric villages are virtually unrepresented by excavations carried out according to modern (post–World War II)
standards. As a result, changes in ecological adaptations or subsistence patterns that might have contributed to the onset of
the Urban Revolution remain on the whole hypothetical. Re-

constructions of individual settlements based on large-scale clearance, to say nothing of regional patterns, are still virtually unknown. What makes this more serious is that non-archeological information, whether from documentary, ethnohistorical, or ethnographic sources, is of very limited importance, since it stems from so much later a time that its applicability is highly questionable.

In comparison with the more three-dimensional picture that complementary sources of data for later periods permit, the prehistoric village record imposes marked limitations or biases. An obvious technological emphasis or even preoccupation, for example, is engendered by the imperishable artifactual materials with which the archeologist generally deals. With the relative paucity of modern excavations in this late preurban time range, the word "artifactual" is an especially appropriate one; on the whole, published illustrations and discussion of wastes of manu-facture (e.g., chipping debris), non-artifactual traces of sub-sistence patterns, and even quantitative data on behavior pat-terns associated with mass-produced artifactual categories are simply unavailable. Disproportionate emphasis also is given to individual objects rather than to complex in situ groupings of features in their architectural context. While archeological pro-cedures for stratigraphic-temporal placement of objects gener-ally have been followed (except in the case of looting, which begins as a significant factor with the later prehistoric time periods), in the absence of quantitative studies the time periods that are assigned tend to be excessively long and impression-istically defined.

From data subject to these limitations, the main outlines of dominant socioeconomic institutions (to say nothing of less tangible aspects of culture) often at best can be only very crudely and conjecturally sketched. In fact, interpretive recon-structions of any kind frequently seem so tenuous that the bulk of what passes for archeological interpretation tends to remain at the level of refinements in time-space systematics—resting

upon the implicit and altogether unwarranted assumption that
the latter are directly equatable with culture process (e.g., the
stale and misleading "diffusion" versus "independent invention"
controversy). Even with all the precision that quantitative archeological techniques of analysis permit under optimal circumstances, of course, chronological controls of the order of two or
three generations remain exceptional. Moreover, work is seldom
possible on a sufficient scale to provide fully equivalent bodies
of material for successive levels.

Under such conditions, accidents of discovery continue to
exercise a decisive influence. This in turn not only supports a
tendency to extreme cautiousness in interpretation but also en-
hances the tendency to "lump" data into larger chronological
categories. As a result, sequences of change are uniformly—and
perhaps quite wrongly—regarded as relatively slow and smoothly
developing rather than rapid and disjunctive. The milieu of research being a largely anthropological one, and archeological
exposures being obviously concentrated on the more important
and long-lived sites, the further tendency has been to interpret
such changes as do appear in the context of community studies
with a strongly localized and integrative focus. Emphasis is
given to objects and institutions evoking consensual patterns of
behavior—art styles, cult objects, rituals—rather than to those
which might suggest incipient patterns of differentiation and
stratification. For all these reasons, the contrast with the politically organized societies of later periods tends to be drawn
as an excessively sharp one, and the onset of the processes of
change comprising the Urban Revolution, as well as the Urban
Revolution itself, tends to be interpreted as more abrupt and
disjunctive than was in fact the case.

There is a broad change in the character of the data with
the onset of the Urban Revolution. Individual settlements characteristically increased in both size and complexity, raising a
host of problems concerned with the representativeness of archeological samples that, at least it is assumed, are distinctly

less important for earlier periods. Monumental buildings, for example, represent at best a small fraction of the spectrum of activities associated with an urban center, but it is equally clear that an archeological reconstruction of urbanism that does not pay them close attention neglects one of the primary symbols, or even a central component, of the Urban Revolution itself. The problem of properly balancing work on monumental structures with other types of excavation, it might be pointed out, is an especially thorny one because of the attraction that temples and palaces have always had for archeologists with individual reputations to establish and museums to fill.

Other sampling problems arise from the trend toward social differentiation. New crafts appeared, each with its own increasingly autonomous and complex techniques and traditions, extending both the material inventory and the range of specialties for which adequate documentation somehow must be supplied from the incomplete and badly preserved record. With increasing social stratification, too, the problem arises whether an individual house or tomb is properly representative of a particular class or status group, so only a vastly expanded number of such features can hope to provide as representative a picture as we assume is available for early villages from more or less random, small-scale exposures.

Finally, urban societies are involved in an unprecedented geographical range of cultural-ecological interactions. Hence, problems of sampling also arise in assessing the role of raw materials brought from great distances or in seeking to evaluate the complementarity of a variety of specialized subsistence sources serving the urban center.

The notorious archeological preoccupation with temples, tombs, and palaces sets its stamp on the interpretation of all later developments that the Urban Revolution inspired. The approach to the study of civilizations characteristically is conducted with big picks and large, inadequately supervised work groups rather than with trowels and paintbrushes primarily

in the hands of students and specialists. As the ratio of specialists to work force and excavated area falls, there is necessarily a radical reduction, on the basis of dubious aesthetic
criteria, in the excavated data that ever are preserved, studied,
and published. And as this reduction implies, there is an increasing preoccupation with narrow, elitist political and cultural traditions in their monumental repositories.

In short, the increasing urgency of the sampling problems
occasioned by the progress of the Urban Revolution is met with
some increase in the scale of exposures but otherwise is only
reinforced by an increasingly arbitrary selectivity. Were we
confined to archeological data of the earlier type alone for the
study of early cities, we would have to acknowledge that there
are increasing sources of distortion whose cumulative effects
upon our capacity to reconstruct cumulative sequences of
change are difficult to estimate but certainly large.

This dismal prognosis fails to materialize because of two
new features: the appearance of writing and the advent of representational art. The latter is much the less important, but it
is also more uniform in its effects upon interpretation and hence
may be considered first. Whether it takes the form of murals or
sculpture, glyptic or ceramics, its content, formal symbolism,
and style in both Mesopotamia and Mesoamerica combine to
suggest for most of it a genesis in myth and ritual rather than
an objective, secular orientation. As such, even though much of
the art portrays individual human protagonists, it reinforces
previously existing biases toward religious institutions and ceremonies.

To be sure, secondary inferences may permit an enhanced
understanding of other social institutions as well—for example,
uniformity and refinement of craftsmanship may suggest the
degree to which full-time specialists were available to be assigned to this aspect of ritual activity, or differences in costume
and other details of portraiture may suggest aspects of the prevailing system of social stratification. But even when that is

possible, art focused on myth and ritual creates special problems of distortion in the study of sociocultural change. It tends to deal mainly with traditionalized, symbolic themes, which probably always were most resistant to change. In so doing, it avoids representation of other activities, particularly in the political and economic sectors, which we might expect to find most sensitive to the trends at the core of the Urban Revolution. Useful and important as representations in art are, therefore, their primary contribution is not to the interpretation of broad institutional patterns but to the fuller understanding of the same limited range of ritualized activities that the remainder of the archeological record already tends to overemphasize.

What saves the situation—indeed, transforms it—is the availability of written evidence. Let us briefly consider its effects for each area. In Mesopotamia, the so-called Protoliterate texts of the terminal fourth millennium B.C. embody a still-primitive system of communication; some of them can be identified as to general subject matter, and individual signs can be identified on the basis of later developments, but translation in the full sense is not possible. With progressive refinements in the cuneiform script during the Early Dynastic period, it emerges by about the middle of the third millennium as a versatile and reasonably unambiguous writing system, however incomplete and imperfect present understandings of it still may be. Hence there was a corresponding expansion in the range of uses to which it is put. By soon after the middle of the third millennium it still consisted, in the main, of massive numbers of briefly noted economic accounts and transactions, but now there also were myths, epics, dynastic lists, syllabaries, land deeds, and royal records which, if not themselves historical in intent, nevertheless provide the basis for reconstructions of political history.

By the later Early Dynastic period of Mesopotamia, the written evidence has immeasurably enlarged and enriched the available archeological record. Phrased differently, archeological evidence begins to serve mainly as loose corroboration for basic patterns of social organization (e.g., social stratification) inferred from texts that take the societal context completely for granted and hence that present it to us only in a very fragmentary fashion. But the opposite approach would not be possible; the unfolding world of social interaction that the documents reveal, even if only fragmentarily as yet, would be forever lost if we had only the archeological record.

Alongside these rich potentialities for interpretation provided by the cuneiform documents, and less often recognized, are distortions that are inherent in the incompleteness of the recovered archives and in the narrowly specialized activities they record. In the first place, the extent of controlled excavations is still minute in relation to even the most important ancient cities. Therefore the written evidence is always fragmentary and tends to be limited to brief chronological intervals at scattered sites, between which synchronisms and direct comparisons are difficult to establish. Also, there is considerable danger that what are interpreted as general conditions in fact may have been of strictly local or temporary application.

There is a second source of error or uncertainty of equal importance. Not merely the literary texts but also those of an economic or administrative character concentrate upon the activities of elite groups and undoubtedly fail to provide a balanced representation even of those. Insofar as the activities of a general public can be perceived at all in such records, they are obviously activities that somehow were important in relation to state institutions; it follows that an accurate assessment of the real importance of such institutions in the lives of ordinary persons is extremely difficult or impossible. Further to obscure the tasks of reconstruction, there is no necessary relationship between the scale or importance of activities and the extent to which it was felt necessary to record them. Not a single account has come to light, for example, of the obviously large and thriving pottery industry that has provided so large a proportion of the grist for all the mills of the archeologists. Or, again, there are virtually innumerable accounts of the receipt or disbursement of grain and animals, but administrative documents dealing with fresh, non-storable vegetables are noteworthy by their absence.[3] What we have, in short, is highly fruitful and often tantalizingly detailed, but we must recognize also that it is highly selective. And, regrettably but not suprisingly, the small class of ancient scribes were not sufficiently detached from their social setting to have left us a description of the principles by which that selection was made.

In Mesoamerica the situation is different. The earliest substantial corpus consists of the inscriptions of the Maya "Classic" period, roughly A.D. 300–900. Thus far only their calendrical aspects have been unequivocally deciphered, although the earlier view that on the whole they were purely of a ritual character is giving way to the belief that they record a substantial amount of political information as well. Pending decipherment, however, they will remain at best a minor resource that is mainly useful in establishing a secure and accurate chronological basis for archeological research in the lowland Maya area.

For the entire remainder of the prehispanic period in Mesoamerica, only a score or so of indigenous documents are known to have survived the destruction—planned as well as merely thoughtless—of the Spanish Conquest. As the accidents of discovery would have it, these are primarily concerned with religion, calendrics, and divination. Of the four large Aztec and three Maya codices known to have been preserved, for example, only one of the former and none of the latter treats historical events. With an acute consciousness of what may have been lost, in other words, we must turn away from indigenous prehispanic sources as a substantial basis for societal interpretation.

What is left are the post-Conquest sources. While internal contradictions and lacunae may abound to the eye of the specialist, the summary impression is of a richness and variety far

3. I am indebted to Miguel Civil for these examples.

surpassing anything available in the Near East. In such accounts of the Conquest itself, for example, as that of Bernal
Díaz or of Cortés in his letters to Charles V, we learn not only
of the death throes of the Mexican state but also much of its
mode of organization in full flower just prior to that time.
Through sixteenth-century Spanish eyes—not the eyes of mod-
erns, to be sure, but far closer to our own time and point of view
than anyone who ever reported on the city-states of early Mesopotamia—we learn of at least the external appearance of an integrated social system functioning over a wide area.

Essentially complementary to this are the encyclopedic compilations of indigenous customs and beliefs compiled by members of Spanish ecclesiastical orders. The great work of Sahagún,
for example, not only sets forth in richly documented detail
the day-to-day life of a wide variety of social strata and specialized groups but also deals comprehensively—if not without
obvious bias—with belief systems and the world of speculative
thought. As an effort at integration and synthesis that is almost
"ethnographic" in scope and intent, again there is absolutely
nothing that remotely approaches it in the entire body of cuneiform literature.

A third major category consists of quasi-historical accounts,
complied and plagiarized, not always critically or disinter-
estedly, by native authors after the Conquest. In these conven-
tionalized and often contradictory accounts of dynastic succession and tribal wanderings the student of Mesopotamian society
would find himself on more familiar ground. Particularly for
periods earlier than the century or less immediately preceding
the Conquest, there is the same problem of separating myth
from history as arises in connection with the early Sumerian
city-states. There is a very similar problem in interdigitating
dynastic lists for separate towns and areas into an intelligible
overall chronology. Still a further common limitation within
which the historian must work in both Mesopotamia and Mesoamerica is the narrowness and somewhat arbitrary quality of

what Leo Oppenheim (1960) has termed the recorded "stream of tradition." Finally, the beginning of the recorded flow is tantalizingly late, particularly in central Mexico where even the immense urban center of Teotihuacán is altogether prehistoric. Given the limited intelligibility of the Protoliterate tablets from Mesopotamia, this situation, too, is relatively similar.

In spite of the similarities of this last category of "historical" writings to those of Mesopotamia, it must be emphasized that the effects of the entire corpus of documentary sources upon an understanding of Mesoamerican society differ sharply from its effects in Mesopotamia. For the synthetic reconstruction of indigenous patterns of political and economic organization in the period immediately prior to the Conquest, we are incomparably better equipped in Mesoamerica than for any period in Mesopotamia. On the other hand, for certain types of quantitative studies, particularly of specialized economic relationships, we are at least potentially in a better position in Mesopotamia. And, more important, the Mesopotamian data permit the study of longer-term developmental trends (at least insofar as they are dependent on documentary sources) than do those in Mesoamerica.

Thus it appears, in summary, that there are real and important factors limiting the comparability of data on the Urban Revolution in Mesopotamia and Mesoamerica. A "contextual" account, as opposed to a more narrowly focused "textual" one, is possible for Mesoamerica during the relatively short span of years immediately preceding the Spanish Conquest. Perhaps the especially full elaboration of the structure and functioning of late prehispanic society owes something also to the anthropological tradition within which much of the data has been studied. But, important as the Spanish sources are, their short time perspective imposes severe limits on interpretation. Above all, it leaves us without an adequate basis on which to assess the rate at which the society was increasing in complexity or coming to be dominated by new institutional patterns. Hence the fundamental cleavage between characterizations of Aztec society as primitive and tribal or advanced and monarchical, dating from the days of Morgan and Bandelier, on the one hand, and Prescott and Bancroft, on the other, remains not fully re-solved today.

Was Tenochtitlán the center of a chiefdom or the capital of a still primitively organized but increasingly formidable em-pire? Surely in the early to mid-*fifteenth* century the former description is correct, but how extensive and basic were the changes during the intervening century before the decapitation of the society at the hands of the Spaniards? Partly, of course, it may be a matter of definitions, but partly also it reflects the ambiguity that arises from the projection of trends across so short and poorly known a period. In any case, for the much longer span of development leading up to the founding of Tula in the tenth century we must depend almost exclusively on the unaided data of archeology, from which developments in the crucial sociopolitical sphere can be inferred only with much effort and considerable uncertainty.

In Mesopotamia, on the other hand, it is the "textual" point of view that predominates in all historical periods. At least partly because of problems inherent in the study of the early cuneiform texts (e.g., the absence of bilingual texts providing translations into fully known languages and the long and com-plex later history of Sumero-Akkadian writing), the purely philological aspects of scholarship that intercede between the student and meaningful problems of sociocultural interpreta-tion are prodigiously more difficult and time-consuming than those in Mesoamerica. Works that genuinely synthesize and analyze the primary textual sources with respect to social in-stitutions are correspondingly rarer and seldom confront one another directly on crucial points of difference. As a degree of compensation, the rate and direction of long-term social trends are at least potentially much better known. Successive steps in the development of social and economic institutions connected with the state are often traceable over many centuries. Here too, however, the crucial early stages of the Urban Revolution lie far back in an essentially prehistoric record, salvageable by archeological means alone.

The shift from almost exclusively archeological evidence at the outset of the Urban Revolution to composite, mutually reinforcing forms of documentation in which texts play an increasing role thus significantly affects interpretation. However, this is not an admission of defeat but only a statement of difficulties to be faced. Similarly, the differences in documentary sources between the Old and the New World are not a justification for eschewing comparison but rather a problem to be recognized and overcome if the comparative outlook claimed for anthropology is more than a pious, meaningless pledge. The broad similarities in the course of the Urban Revolution in a number of historically independent areas, and in the organization of the primitive states that were its culminating products, simply demand recognition and study as essentially parallel examples of a particular type of development in a "multilinear" evolutionary framework.

As Julian Steward has put it, what is necessary is that "comparative cultural studies should interest themselves in recurrent phenomena as well as in unique phenomena, and that anthropology explicitly recognizes that a legitimate and ultimate objective is to see through the differences of cultures to the similarities, to ascertain processes that are duplicated independently in cultural sequences, and to recognize cause and effect in both temporal and functional relationships" (1955:180). It is with the detailed discussion of these questions, as they apply in the specific cases of Mesopotamia and central Mexico, that the remainder of this study deals.

II

SUBSISTENCE AND SETTLEMENT

IT IS A TRUISM THAT COMPLEX, CIVILIZED SOCIETIES DEPEND UPON a subsistence base that is sufficiently intensive and reliable to permit sedentary, nucleated settlements, a circumstance that under most circumstances, and certainly in the long run, has implied agriculture.

A significant exception to that generalization may have occurred in restricted regions of the Near East during and soon after the closing phases of the Pleistocene. Recently Jean Perrot has argued that the evidence for either plant or animal domesticates in Palestine and Syria remains at best highly ambiguous until possibly as late as the fifth millennium B.C., in spite of the fact that a settlement like Jericho already had become a small walled town or village as early as the eighth millennium (1964: 18). In this case, of course, the major resources would have been the wild progenitors of the later domesticated races of wheat, barley, sheep, and goats, supplemented by a greater quantity and variety of wild plant foods and lacustrine products than is available in the region today. Probably even the wild cereals alone, einkorn, emmer, and two-row barley, were a larger and more stable subsistence resource than commonly has been realized. Recent experiments indicate[1] that yields of as much as 40 kilograms per family per day of actual grain equivalents over a three-week harvest period are still possible on unprotected Near Eastern stands of wild einkorn, suggesting that the

1. Jack R. Harlan, personal communication.

harvest of wild grain could even have been the basic subsistence resource, at least within the relatively limited (and not identical!) ecological niches where conditions for each of the plants were favorable.

But the important point is that these conditions seemingly were transitory and passed on without having generated civilized, urban societies. The early florescence represented by "neolithic" Jericho was followed in that area by widespread abandonments, and settled life, when it reappeared in that area and apparently even upon its first appearance elsewhere, was and thenceforth remained agricultural.

The domestication of cereals immensely expanded the environmental range within which these crops were an effective subsistence source, and it surely also increased substantially the size and reliability of yields in relation both to labor input and to available land. As the numbers and range of sheep and goats also expanded following their domestication, an assured supply of milk and meat products came to overlap the expanding ranges of distribution of the cereals, further establishing the superiority of agriculture. It was upon this basis, although with such important later additions as cattle, pigs, donkeys, and the domesticated date palm, that early Mesopotamian civilization met its underlying subsistence needs.

In Mesoamerica, the pattern was somewhat different. The wild progenitors of the great New World triad of food plants, especially maize but also beans and squash, required a much longer period of selective breeding before they became sufficient, as domesticates, to replace a wide spectrum of hunted and gathered products. Fully sedentary village life accordingly began much later than in the Old World, perhaps even as late as the middle of the first millennium B.C., although the earliest incipient cultivation extends back into at least the seventh millennium.

Perhaps the very limited role of domesticable animals—only the dog and turkey ever became economically important out-

side Peru—contributed to this retardation by failing to provide
inducements to an agricultural mode of subsistence as compel-
ling as those that had been present in the Old World. Hus-
bandry, for example, permitted the involvement of even quite
young children in the productive process as herdsmen, thus
perhaps stimulating population growth. It also created special
opportunities for enhanced resource utilization, as exemplified
by stubble-grazing and consequent manuring.

For purposes of understanding the Urban Revolution, however, differences in the onset of food production between the
Old and the New World are of little consequence, except insofar as they reflect cumulative differences in subsistence potentialities. What matters are the underlying similarities in the
conditions precipitating the Food-Producing Revolution, as well
as in the major changes of which it was constituted. For these,
it now seems clear, identify the Food-Producing Revolution not
merely as the predecessor and prerequisite for the Urban Revolution but as a type of transformation profoundly different
from the latter.

As I have argued elsewhere, the closing phases of the Pleistocene saw a whole series of adaptive changes in subsistence, of
which the incipient development of agriculture at first was only
a regional variant (Adams 1693). Perhaps foremost among the
more general features of the changes was an increasing seden-
tism, based upon the substitution of patterns of intensive localized, "broad-spectrum" collecting for the more wide-ranging
selective pursuit of migratory herbivores. These localized patterns took many forms, ranging from new techniques for the
exploitation of riverine and lacustrine resources to a fuller and
more variegated reliance on seeds, fruits, nuts, and small forest
animals. Many, if not most, of the new patterns involved the
development of a new technology as well: composite tools and
weapons like drills and bows, more specialized reaping and digging tools than had been necessary earlier, grinding stones for
extracting seeds from husks, cooking processes suitable for the

new task of making vegetal foods edible and palatable in bulk, not to mention even more ambitious devices, such as boats, nets, weirs, and their associated equipment, which were necessary for the successful exploitation of shoreline environments. It is apparent that much of this technological advance is "preadapt-ive" for successful agriculture, which even in cultural terms consists of hardly anything more profound than the intentional sowing or breeding of plants and animals whose exploitation for food must already have been well known. Moreover, it has recently been pointed out that from an ecological standpoint the distinction between terminal food-collecting and the onset of food production is equally elusive and artificial:

. . . the important point is not that man *planted* wheat but that he (i) moved it to niches to which it was not adapted, (ii) re-moved certain pressures of natural selection, which allowed more deviants from the normal phenotype to survive, and (iii) eventually selected for characters not beneficial under conditions of natural selection [Flannery 1965:1251].

In short, the Food-Producing Revolution was a "process" and not an "event," in that it developed gradually or by small steps over a considerable period and followed different emphases and sequences according to differing local conditions even within the Near East and Mesoamerica.

What were the essential features of agriculture, not only as a mode of subsistence but as a set of social problems and ac-tivities, which seem to have influenced the course of the Urban Revolution? We may begin with certain very general conse-quences of food production that tend to be common to all its manifestations, and then turn subsequently to those whose effects may have been at least partly different in Mesopotamia and in Mesoamerica.

Increased yields, in relations to labor input, have already been mentioned. An essential feature of virtually every agricul-tural regime is that its demands upon the farmer are discontinu-ous through the year and, moreover, are generally phased fairly uniformly for the population of an entire region. This provides a basis not merely for a substantially greater aggregate of leisure time than most hunting-collecting societies can achieve but also for its organized disposition as labor not directly tied to the satisfaction of the immediate subsistence requirements of the primary producers and their families—and hence for the control and manipulation of labor as a form of capital.

Figures are obviously variable according to local conditions, particularly in Mesoamerica, but under the traditional swidden agricultural regime a representative published estimate of annually required labor ranges from 143 to 161 man-days at Tepoztlán, including time required for fencing against cattle (not a prehispanic problem) and providing substantial surpluses available for sale. In Mesopotamia the local differences probably are less significant, but the problem of obtaining estimates is obscured by oppressive conditions of tenancy. In general, however, the same impression of substantial potential leisure is confirmed. Recent calculations from the northern part of the alluvial plain suggest that maximally there are about 249 man-days of agricultural labor per family unit per year under the traditional methods of cultivation, with the immediate subsistence requirements of the producing family of peasants seemingly needing only half or less of this time investment. In both cases, to be sure, it should be noted that the estimates include only the work of the men in the fields and in crop transport. To this must be added the frequently onerous and always time-consuming tasks of fuel collection and food preparation, the former also men's work, at least in modern Mexico, while in contemporary Iraq both fall to women.

As to yields in relation to land, the virtue of agriculture is not so much in its higher potential value over that for hunting-collecting under ideal local conditions as it is in the aggregate number of units in a relatively large area that can maintain substantial and roughly equivalent outputs. In this sense, agriculture can be said to constitute an artificial extension of the ecological niche available for certain cultigens through such techniques as weeding, clearing, seeding, and irrigation, an extension that permits immensely larger population aggregates in suitable areas. Of course, it remains an empirical question whether great size and density of rural population were a precondition for the growth of nucleated, urban settlements or whether, instead, the progress of the Urban Revolution provided a profound inducement to the growth of the rural population as well.

Representative figures for land requirements for subsistence in Mesoamerica again tend to be highly variable according to local conditions and type of agriculture. Under the traditional swidden or "slash-and-burn" system in the forested tropical lowlands, from 7.5 to 15 or more hectares per family are required either under cultivation or as part of a cyclically utilized reserve. In the highlands, the maintenance of permanent kitchen gardens in addition to the practice of swidden has been reported to reduce land requirements to perhaps 6.5 hectares per family. Where there is irrigation, these figures are much more radically reduced—to less than a hectare where alternate rainfall and irrigation permit two crops to be harvested per year and to less than half a hectare under the especially intensive conditions of chinampa cultivation around the lakes in the Valley of Mexico. For Mesopotamia, there are no adequate data available on maximal yields attainable with irrigation. Since shortages of water limit the land that can be cultivated, there is little incentive to maximize output per unit area; hence cultivation has always been extensive rather than intensive, with single crop cultivation during the winter growing season and with alternate years in fallow. Even on this basis, however, a recent report indicates that in one district the median holding of farm-owning families was 6 hectares. Presumably minimal requirements for subsistence are considerably less than this figure.

A third concomitant of agricultural subsistence related to

the growth of civilization was increased stability of residence. Data on this subject would depend on kinds of longitudinal studies that are seldom undertaken even by modern ethnographers and that are essentially unavailable in ancient records or in archeological findings. But surely we are justified in assuming that agriculture generally is a strong inducement to at least relative stability and that residential stability in turn is positively associated with an increasing technological repertoire. Perhaps as important as its effect on the development of new tools and specialized skills, residential stability may also engender social stability, encouraging an irregular but cumulative shift from small lineage-oriented systems in which fissionary tendencies dominate to larger, more open-ended systems tending toward local continuity and endogamy.

Certain built-in incentives to population growth constitute a fourth feature of agricultural regimes generally and, presumably, of those in early Mesopotamia and Mesoamerica as well. Children, for example, can be incorporated into the productive process earlier than is the case among hunter-gathers. More important, since agriculture constitutes not merely the passive exploitation of an existing ecological niche but an expansion of it, the number and size of agricultural communities in a given region can grow substantially without increasing the pressure upon their resource base; on the other hand, such pressures tend to increase on hunter-gatherers as population increases.

The foregoing is not meant to imply that population increases that are due to agriculture set the stage for urbanization. Possibly the attainment of some minimal population level was necessary to set the process into motion. But such evidence as there is suggests that appreciable population increases generally followed, rather than preceded, the core processes of the Urban Revolution. Particularly in Mesopotamia, where the sedentary village pattern seems to have been stabilized for several millennia between the establishment of effective food production and the "take-off" into urbanism, it may be noted that there is simply no evidence for gradual population increases that might have helped to precipitate the Urban Revolution after reaching some undefined threshold. Given the nature of the evidence available at present, of course, it must be added that any attempt to describe the extent or timing of demographic changes in relation to the Urban Revolution in both Mesopotamia and Mesoamerica remains hazardous in the extreme.

Next we may consider the nature of agricultural "surpluses" insofar as they may have been a precondition for the Urban Revolution in Mesopotamia and Mesoamerica. That agricultural producers can, to a degree quite unprecedented among hunters and collectors, be induced or compelled to provide a surplus above their own subsistence needs for socially defined ends is little more than a truism. But does the exploitation of a given environment by a given agricultural technology, implying a potential level of productivity from which actual consumption can be subtracted to define the surplus available for reallocation, actually help to engender the ideologies and institutional contexts that are required to mobilize that surplus? Is there an inherent tendency for agriculturalists to advance in productivity toward the highest potential level consistent with their technology, that is, to maximize their production above subsistence needs and so to precipitate the growth of new patterns of appropriation and consumption involving elites freed from responsibilities for food production? Gordon Childe, although never dealing with these issues directly, appears to have thought so. Karl Polanyi and his collaborators have argued persuasively to the contrary (1957), noting that actual agricultural surpluses are always defined and mobilized in a particular institutional setting and that it is precisely the growth of the collective symbols and institutions of the primitive states that can explain the conversion of peasant leisure into foodstuffs in urban storehouses.

A useful and somewhat different approach to the problem of interpreting the significance of agricultural surpluses has recently been suggested by Martin Orans (1966). Briefly, he focuses criticism on the conception of surplus as it is applied at the level of the individual producer. What really matters, he argues, is not the margin between per capita production and consumption, which implies improving "efficiency" as the major factor in change and which is inherently incalculable from the usual archeological-historical data. At least from the viewpoint of understanding sociocultural change, the crucial variable, instead, is the *gross* amount of deployable wealth or "surplus."

There are several advantages to conceptualizing the problem in these terms. First, it calls attention to the fact that a chain of processes is involved in mobilizing "surpluses" in any sociocultural context rather than merely the attainment of a margin between production and consumption on the part of the primary producers. The accumulation of a surplus is at least facilitated by improvements in technological-transport facilities not directly related to agriculture at all (e.g., boats and carts) and, in any case, involves the elaboration of complex institutional mechanisms, not merely for assuring production of a surplus by the peasantry, but also for concentrating and reallocating it. Equally important, the concept of gross surplus directs attention to the political or religious centers of the society, urban or otherwise. It was in those centers, after all, that its utilization resulted in the formation of the new classes and groups of specialists, as well as the monumental structures and luxuries primarily associated with them, by which we identify the Urban Revolution in the first place.

Emphasis on gross surplus rather than per capita surplus serves other functions as well. It suggests, for example, that an increase in the gross size of population and territorial unit may offer *at least* as strong a stimulus to the Urban Revolution as putative increases in "efficiency." Trends toward territorial aggrandizement, political unification, and population concentration within the political unit accordingly can be interpreted not merely as expressions of the outcome of the Urban Revolution but as functionally interrelated processes that are central to it.

Calculated as gross amounts of deployable wealth rather than per capita ones, the significance of surpluses changes from an implied independent factor of change to a component in an interdependent network of cause and effect. Extensions of territorial control, new forms of political superordination, and a multiplicity of technological advances all may have had as much effect on the size of the surplus as improvements in immediate agricultural "efficiency," while the deployment of the surplus, however it was formed, obviously had important reciprocal effects on these other factors. Further to emphasize the interdependency of surpluses with a host of political, economic, and technological institutions, it may be noted that agriculture received organizational inputs from some of the institutions that emerged during the course of the Urban Revolution. At least in the case of Mesopotamia, rationalization of production in large-scale, internally specialized units surely increased not only gross output but also per capita productivity, suggesting that surpluses can be isolated from the processes constituting the Urban Revolution as a whole only in the sense that they may serve as convenient indices for it. In reality, they and the institutions promoting and disposing of them were inextricably intertwined to form its substance.

The composite character of both Mesopotamian and Mesoamerican subsistence patterns is a somewhat less easily defined and tangible common feature that nevertheless seems certain to be functionally related to the onset of the Urban Revolution. Phrased differently, there were significant respects in both cases in which their component producing units were not self-sustaining. While specific forms naturally differed greatly, some of the most characteristic institutions of the emergent states in both areas played a decisive role in mediating the relationship between the complementarily specialized units of production.

This point may be more fully explained by considering each of the areas separately.

While from a distance the Mesopotamian alluvium appears to be an ecologically undifferentiated region, in fact there always have been a number of distinctively specialized subsistence zones within it. Wheat and barley cultivation is perhaps the best known, with the prevailing emphasis on the latter being related to the fluctuating effects of salinity. It takes the form of field cultivation on an extensive rather than intensive basis, both along levee back-slopes and the margins of swamps and depressions. A second niche consists of garden and orchard cultivation. These summer harvests are small, limited to 10 per cent or less of the areas devoted to the winter cereals by the sharply reduced availability of water; hence they are largely confined to favorable low-lying areas adjoining permanent watercourses. A third adaptation is that of the herdsman, including weeds and stubble in fallow fields (establishing a pattern of symbiosis with cultivators), as well as great enclosed or marginal tracts of semiarid pastureland. Fourth, the swamps and rivers constitute a subsistence system whose importance is often neglected, serving as the source of reeds, one of the few locally available building materials outside the soil itself, and also of fish. Fish constituted perhaps the major source of protein in the southern Mesopotamian diet; its importance as an economic activity is suggested by the fact that more than 100 of the 1,200 or so members of the Bau community in Early Dynastic Lagash are listed in contemporary texts as fishermen, and 125 more as oarsmen, pilots, longshoremen, and sailors.

The important point about these subsistence alternatives is that they were pursued by specialists in whose activities and interrelations the formal organizations of the community played a substantial intervening role. In the case of cultivators, for example, we learn from the tablets of ancient Shuruppak that both seed and plow animals were often centrally maintained, supplied, and accounted for. As many as 9,660 donkeys are accounted for on one Early Dynastic administrative text alone, and the responsibility for plowing, even on private land, seems to have rested with corvées under the direction of appointive officials. Significantly, signs apparently referring to plowing officials can be recognized on Protoliterate texts representing temple accounts, so this centralization is as old as our earliest written evidence.

With respect to herding, the involvement of the central institutions of the city was as decisive as in the case of farming. It is suggested by the preoccupation of so much of the early glyptic art with sacred herds and by the substantial temple and palace holdings of domesticated animals recorded on Early Dynastic texts. Or, to refer again to the Bau texts from Early Dynastic Lagash, almost 100 members of that community were listed as specialized herdsmen. Perhaps the problem of sparse summer forage was a particularly critical one, necessitating centralized management, particularly in the case of the larger bovids and equids, but in addition part of the explanation surely lies in the importance of wool for the manufacture of textiles upon which the long-distance trade for needed raw materials like copper must have depended.

Another part of the domain of the herdsmen lay outside the perimeters of cultivation and settlement, depending on open, semiarid steppes for the sustenance of migratory herds rather than on young barley shoots or stubble in cultivated fields. But, although the nomads occupying the region may have been able to resist political ties with the scattered enclaves of urban settlement and irrigation agriculture in their midst, in a more important sense they remained a vital part of an interacting cultural and economic whole. Recently it has been noted, for example, that the great early centers of the cult of the shepherd god, Dumuzi, lay in cities bordering the Sumerian edin or pasturing ground.

Similarly in the case of the fishermen, the central institutions of the emergent Sumerian city-states played an active role with respect to both their production and their consumption patterns. The so-called "mashdaria" texts from Lagash, for example, have been interpreted for many years as reflecting very large "offerings" of fish by the fishermen to the temple—offerings so large that their further employment for food by a large part of the working force of the temple community has generally been taken for granted. Insofar as these texts deal with "offerings" at all, there are indications that they refer to contributions made to the exchequer of the ruler and his family, from which in turn we may assume they were redistributed. But probably it would be more accurate to conclude that they deal with a form of ritualized interchange, carefully accounted for by the officials of the Bau community, in which herdsmen and fishermen exchanged milk products and fish with each other and for cloth. And it should be remembered that the large quantities of fishbones reported to have been found in late Ubaid temple levels at Eridu point to a very early beginning of ritualized patterns of either offering or exchange in which at least the products of the specialized group of fishermen were made available to a considerably wider segment of the population.

A still more direct and basic form of interchange of subsistence products is attested by numerous Early Dynastic and Akkadian texts. It consisted of large-scale distributions of rations to dependents of the great state institutions. The complexity of this system, with regard both to the commodities involved and to the gradations of support that were extended to different age, occupational, and social groups, recently have been adumbrated by I. J. Gelb (1965). Presumably in exchange for corresponding periods of labor service by productive adult workers, the system made allowance for the aged and even for nursing infants. At least among the parishioners of the large landed demesnes, the allotment of subsistence plots thus was importantly supplemented by the issuance of monthly rations of barley—for varying periods of the year, depending upon political conditions as well as upon degrees of dependency. In addition, there were annual rations of oil and wool, as well as distributions at festivals and, on other special occasions, of mutton, beef and fish, dairy products, vegetables, dates and other fruits, and beer and wine.

In short, the subsistence patterns of late fourth and early third millennium B.C. Mesopotamia involve specialized groups of producers whose relations were characteristically mediated by the dominant urban institutions, including the palace and the temple. Although a quantitative summary has not yet been attempted (and indeed may be meaningless until a wider selection of contemporary Early Dynastic archives is available), the general outline of the system conforms strikingly well to the "redistributive" model that Polanyi and his collaborators have sketched; moreover, there are at least hints in the available data that the actual flow of goods and services was large in relation to the total available supply of such goods and services. Surely we see here, as was adumbrated earlier, not merely a complex pattern of subsistence but one in which the interdependence of its component features played a material part in shaping the institutions by which we identify the Urban Revolution itself.

The Mesoamerican pattern was different in important ways and yet generically similar. There were densely settled enclaves where conditions were favorable for continuous or intensive agriculture with the indigenous crops and technology, separated from one another by extremely rugged areas, permitting, at best, marginal settlement. Differences in rainfall, in soils, and, above all, in elevation, profoundly affected the complex of cultivable crops upon which depended not only trade in luxuries but also some commodities closely linked with subsistence. Regionally adapted varieties of maize, to be sure, grew in virtually every habitable zone, but chiles and maguey, the latter an important source of amino acids in diets generally low in protein, were specialized highland products. Cotton and cacao beans, on the other hand, were cultivated only at lesser elevations, the former having already been imported into the great central valley of Mexico long before the Christian Era, while the latter had become the accepted medium of interregional exchange by the Postclassic period, if not earlier. Salt, obtained particularly along the seacoasts, was another important commodity of trade. Perhaps most significant as a specialized subsistence zone was the Valley of Mexico, occupying only an insignificant proportion of the Mesoamerican gross land area but supporting highly productive chinampa horticulture and providing a rich lacustrine fauna as well.

This regional contrast, and the prevailing symbiosis that it encouraged, constituted an "ecological mosaic," as it has been called, of strikingly different and yet interdependent zones of specialization. The pattern as a whole was similar to Mesopotamia in its high degree of internal differentiation, and, as in Mesopotamia, it is not unreasonable to suppose that some of the most advanced and characteristic institutions of Mesoamerican society were centrally involved, and may even have had their origins, in mediating the relationships and interchanges between the specialized components.

Further, one of the profound differences between the early state societies of Mesopotamia and Mesoamerica may lie in the particular local features that this complexity assumed. In Mesopotamia distances were small, geographical barriers were unimportant, and interaction between those engaged in different subsistence pursuits was close, many-faceted, and continuous. Most communities, accordingly, were composite with regard to subsistence specializations, and the responsibility of religious and political authorities in relation to subsistence was to maintain and improve a system of relationships already existing within their boundaries. At least down through the Akkadian period and perhaps somewhat later, the careful management and recording of a system for the redistribution of subsistence products in the form of rations was the central economic activity and concern of the state institutions. The institution of the marketplace, with ancillary jural and ceremonial features, was largely or entirely absent.

In Mesoamerica, on the other hand, only the relatively less deep-rooted "imperial" polities like that of the Aztecs might be said to have transcended the limitations of a single geographical (mainly altitudinal) zone, and a dominant orientation of the urban elites lay in the promotion of "external" trade. Hence it is not surprising that upon their arrival in central Mexico the Spaniards found the institution of the marketplace in hyper-developed form; 60,000 persons, for example, were daily in attendance at the market in Tlatelolco, and 30,000 even in a much smaller principality like Tlaxcala. Large-scale trade by barter is reported not only in luxuries but in virtually all sub-sistence products, clothing, and even rudimentary agricultural implements, and there were elaborate juridical institutions for maintaining market norms. By as early as the middle of the first millennium A.D. at Teotihuacán, there are suggestions that great marketplaces had emerged as architectual establishments with well-defined internal arrangements. All these are features that are missing in Mesopotamia.

A further general similarity between Mesopotamian and Mesoamerican subsistence patterns, again accompanied by re-gionally variable forms whose differences are also significant for our purposes, is an increasing intensity of land use. Best known among the patterns of ecological modification to which this refers is the introduction of irrigation, and there seems little reason to doubt that it was generally accompanied by at least a relative increase in the productivity of lands under cultivation. But in one sense the term "intensity" is perhaps a misleading one. It implies a special emphasis upon labor-intensive tech-niques of agriculture in which the productivity of a fixed, limited amount of agricultural land rises in direct proportion to a spiraling labor input. Something of the kind can indeed be discerned on an extremely limited scale in the chinampa horti-culture practiced in the Valley of Mexico, but there is no evidence that it ever was a widespread, general feature of either central Mexican or Mesopotamian agriculture.

A better way of characterizing these modified patterns of land use, at least in terms of the changes in social organization they may have brought about, involves not their productivity in relation to land area or labor input but their unstabilizing effect upon communal systems of land tenure and the consequent inducement they provide to the growth of social stratification. Irrigation systems, for example, are capital investments that enhance the productivity of the tracts and groups they serve but not others. Given inadequacies in water supply (whether arising from a limited average supply in relation to land, from year-to-year fluctuations, or from lack of congruence between maximum stream flow and the growing season), the usual condition in both Mesopotamia and Mesoamerica, such systems represent relatively permanent improvements, which restrict or distort uniformity of access to the primary productive resources of the community and which tend to concentrate the potentialities for the production of a surplus of deployable wealth in the hands of a limited social segment. Depending on local circumstances, such potentialities may be reckoned in terms of rights to land or to water, but the effect is the same in either case. They stimulate the concentration of hereditable, alienable wealth in productive resources, and hence also the emergence of a class society

Such, at least, is the pattern that can be followed in some ethnographic examples, for example, Ralph Linton's account of the introduction of wet rice cultivation in Madagascar (1939). In Sinhalese villages, on the other hand, Edmund Leach reports that such effects can be held in check for long periods within the community by internal leveling mechanisms based upon periodic fractionation and redistribution of holdings (1961). Given such diametrically opposed alternatives, our question becomes: Under the particular conditions present in early Mesopotamia and Mesoamerica were the disequilibrating effects of patterns of differential land use somehow held in check or were they instead an important inducement to the growth of a stratified society? In both cases there is good evidence for a decisive increase in social stratification; before dealing with it, however, we should examine the possible roots of the process in the prevailing subsistence patterns.

In Mesopotamia the problem of ecological inducements to social stratification is both complex and obscure. There are abundant records, from Protoliterate times on, of great differences in ownership of land or rights to its usufruct. But it has not yet been possible to position these early holdings with respect to one another, to establish the relationship between purchase price and yield for the same fields, or to show how closely the very large holdings coincided with superior soils, access to irrigation water, and productivity. Seemingly, all that we can fall back on at present are some indirect and rather doubtful hints.

First, the rate of seeding in late Early Dynastic times was exceedingly low—only a sixth or seventh of contemporary Western practice, although not greatly different from contemporary practice in the same area. This low seeding rate, together with reliance on a simple system of fallow rotation throughout antiquity (and, for the most part, up until the present), suggests prevailingly extensive rather than intensive cultivation. However, it does not rule out the possibility that there were substantial relative differences in the value of arable lands, since under the traditional agricultural regime a low seeding rate is ecologically advantageous (it provides a measure of protection against water shortages, as well as higher proportionate yields in relation to a given volume of applied water). Such differences are confirmed by the fact that in a number of cases the purchase price is differentiated into a component directly based on land area and a supplemental charge for capital improvements or extras like a standing crop or adjacent canals. Indeed, pre-Sargonic purchase prices for land range rather widely—between factors of one and six times per given unit of surface area, clearly suggesting important differences in productivity, ease of access, assurance of adequate irrigation water, devotion to intensive orchard cultivation, or the like.

In spite of this considerable variability, the price of land in the Early Dynastic sale texts is prevailingly low, generally corresponding to no more than might be harvested from it over a two- or three-year period and on occasion less than even a single year's harvest. This low land price seems to confirm the existence of a relatively non-intensive system of cultivation, with greatly excessive areas of potentially cultivable land in relation to the available supplies of irrigation water, but, of course, may mean little, since it is not known *what* proportion of *which* fields are referred to in the existing sale texts—whether marginally irrigated or well supplied with water. It is entirely possible that the more favorably situated lands constituted large, growing holdings in the hands of elites; if so, they would seldom be formally transferred and hence recorded.

Somewhat surprisingly, in view of the critical scarcity of water rather than land, rights of ownership apparently were calculated exclusively in land and not in water, which must reflect the wide variations in flow of the major streams, their tendency to shift their courses, and the difficulties of measuring water consumption. There is also a noteworthy absence among the literary sources—proverbs, disputations, etc.—of references to controversies over water rights, such as might be expected if there were gross, permanent inequalities in access rights to this critical resource. And, similarly, the early references to the construction of canal systems generally specify their importance as arteries of communication and do not mention at all the water they provided for irrigation.

The large corpus of texts touching on the agricultural economy also contains little to indicate the development on a significant scale of any more intensive type of land use than the traditional system of fallow rotation, which suggests no very marked trend to increase field productivity even on favorably situated tracts. On the other hand, it leaves unexplained the substantial differences in the unit costs for land. Finally, the role of the corporate landholding groups that are in evidence in Early Dynastic times subsequently seems to be a progressively more restricted one, and no mechanisms for periodic land redistribution within such groups, which might have prolonged their survival by reducing internal differentiation, are directly attested in the available record.[2]

What emerges from this miscellany of observations is that agriculture remained overwhelmingly extensive rather than intensive and that there is little or no evidence of intracommunity competition over scarce land and water resources. Thus, while all our evidence points to increasing inequalities in the control of deployable wealth, the available evidence from ancient texts neither proves nor disproves that they were significantly enhanced by locally emerging patterns of differentiation in subsistence control or productivity. Of course, such inequalities were increasingly *reflected* in differences in landownership, as the great acquisitions by single individuals that are recorded in Early Dynastic texts clearly show. But, while wide variations in sizes of holdings may have perpetuated, or even intensified, the process of social stratification as a whole, it simply cannot be shown directly how much of that variation was an outcome of trends inherent in the local subsistence system.

Even if unambiguous contemporary evidence is still lacking, however, a consideration of the ecological circumstances characteristic of the Mesopotamian plain strongly suggests that increasing disproportions in the control of deployable wealth were at least partly induced by the local subsistence system. It

2. On the other hand, Miguel Civil suggests (personal communication) that the extremely long and narrow shape of fields recorded in somewhat later (Ur III) texts may imply impermanent boundaries between individual allotments within larger corporate holdings.

cannot be overstressed that traditional irrigation agriculture in that context is maintained within at best an *unstable* eco-system. Great variations in rainfall and river flow, silting, increasing salinity with rising groundwater levels, periodic infestations by blights and insect pests, the delicately shifting balance between nomads and settled peoples—all are repeatedly attested throughout the historical record and are still in evidence today. Considered in relation to human settlement, in vulnerable, narrow enclaves along shifting, inadequate watercourses, such factors leading to marked differences in the control of productive land and agricultural surpluses have always been overwhelming and chronic.

While these processes are perhaps most obvious among cultivators, Frederik Barth's work on the nomadic Basseri of southwestern Iran provides a paradigm that must have obtained among ancient Mesopotamian herdsmen as well (Barth 1961). Barth emphasizes that nomadic life is not to be understood as an isolate but that, instead, there is a continuing dependence upon neighboring zones of cultivation. One form of this dependence, and perhaps the primary one for our purposes, is that there is a continuing feedback of population into the settlements. In part it consists of a relatively large proportion of the nomadic population whose herds for one reason or another fall below the minimal level necessary to maintain extended family groups. Such groups have no recourse but to trickle into the cultivated zones as a disorganized, depressed, landless labor force. A smaller, but for our purposes equally important, upper stratum of nomads is successful in increasing its ratio of animals to herdsmen past the point at which it is economical to manage them. This stratum must seek to convert its herds into a more stable form of capital, and specifically into land that can be maintained in production either by the former herdsman and some of his followers or on an absentee basis. Even without considering the political effects of large groupings of nomads, in other words, we can identify potent disequilibrating factors arising from the symbiotic interaction of herdsmen and farmers that must always have been reflected in tendencies toward increasing inequalities in landholdings.

As the example of herdsman-cultivator symbiosis testifies, ecological relationships that were significant for the growth of social stratification are not necessarily understood best from the standpoint of the nucleated community. The network of signficant ecological relationships need not be coterminous with the self-conscious territorial, social, or religious unit. Granting the biases and limitations of the contemporary sources, what they attest is not so much the onset of processes of social differentiation within communities as the existence of prolonged and bitter intercommunity struggles. In most cases such struggles may have had their origins in subsistence practices or requirements, for example, the opposing demands of upstream and downstream irrigators, rival claims to adjacent lands, or the characteristically divergent local patterns of substantial surplus and impoverishment. But they clearly are to be understood in a regional rather than an intracommunity framework. Whatever their initial roots, rivalries of this kind lead to consolidations of land, population, and agricultural surplus in which political and economic factors were closely intertwined. Thus externally imposed patterns of political and military domination are an important facet of the development of social differentiation, complementing its emergence as a result of ecological pressures within the community.

There is an additional reason for considering the adaptive patterns characteristic of Mesopotamia as regional in scope rather than as centering upon an individual sedentary community. Mesopotamian herdsmen and farmers, or rural folk and city-dwellers, for the most part have never been fully stable types but a shifting continuum. Particularly in early times, the self-conscious, committed urban elite was extraordinarily thin, a relative handful of administrators, priests, scribes, and perhaps craftsmen in a population among most of whom settled city life was continuously viewed as merely one of several available alternatives. Although Leo Oppenheim was concerned primarily with later periods in a recent discussion of this theme, there is no reason to doubt that his account is equally applicable to the city-states of the Early Dynastic and Akkadian periods:

The palace, of course, the temple, and the hard core of city-dwellers in the large and old cities had only occasional contacts with the people in the open country, who subsisted on the yield of this environment and were not to be forced into sedentary conditions. Between these two groups there were important fluctuations comprising smaller or larger segments of the population of the cities as well as the open country. Difficult economic and political situations were liable to crowd out of the cities such persons as delinquent debtors, power groups defeated in intracity striving, defectors from the great organizations, and others. In the open country, they joined the inhabitants of abandoned villages and settlements who had been driven into a seminomadic way of life by the deterioration of the soil, the breakdown of facilities for irrigation, or because they had rebelled against taxes and rents. The number of these was increased by infiltrating groups from the mountains and the deserts around Mesopotamia. Thus the ranks of this fluctuating element of the population could swell at times of crisis to a dangerous degree, even engulfing the cities, and—if led by an energetic and efficient political or military leader—it could transfer the rule over the city, and even that over the entire country, into the hands of outsiders or newcomers. Whenever linguistic differences appear between the city and such power groups in the rebellious hinterlands, or more exactly, between the dialect used to write official documents in the city and that actually spoken by the group in command, we have the impression of sudden foreign invasions, bringing kings bearing foreign names to the throne. Such dramatic changes need not have been the result, necessarily, of foreign invasion but could have been brought about by a rather slow economic and political process of increasing social unrest which would not be reflected in extant documents. The most effective remedy against these potentially dangerous elements were projects of internal and frontier colonization which only a powerful king could set afoot. The inscriptions of such kings speak triumphantly of the ingathering . . . of the scattered, the resettling . . . of the shiftless on new land, where the king forced them to dig or re-dig canals, build or resettle cities, and till the soil, pay taxes, do corvée work to maintain the irrigation system, and—last but not least—perform military service [1964:82–83].

Parallels between the process that Oppenheim describes and the relationships between city-dwellers in central Mexico and the so-called Chichimecs along the northern periphery of Meso-american settlement are immediately apparent. The ecological frontier of farming in the latter region repeatedly failed to coincide with the cultural frontier, so marginal groups must have shifted back and forth from farming to nomadic hunting and collecting as the political authority and prosperity of the great urban centers at their rear waxed and waned. The traditional accounts tend to speak of the Chichimecs as invaders exclusively from beyond the *limes* of civilization, responsible for the fall of cities through their unaided military pressure. Given the limited numbers and resources of nomads and their necessarily high degree of dispersal, this explanation seems most unlikely; Pedro Armillas (1964a) has very recently demolished such an interpretation in detail. It is the characteristic "urban" distortion of a complex, dynamic relationship and bears a close analogy to, for example, the Chinese or Arab attributions of overwhelming strength and destructiveness to their Mongol invaders. The decisive forces, in fact, were the marginal cultivators within the ambit of political and religious influences emanating from the major centers, for to them slight environmental shifts (for which Armillas argues) and increases in nomadic pressure could upset a sensitive balance and precipitate a widespread withdrawal from patterns of peaceful settlement.

Under the conditions of territorial expansion and firm political control that seemingly obtained at the time of the Toltec "empire," for example, there is evidence that the zone of settlement not only reached its outermost continuous limits but jumped beyond them to form a series of isolated enclaves of local irrigation extending northward for hundreds of miles in the narrow ecological niche formed by the junction between the hot steppe and the mesothermal savannah belt. With the internal collapse of Toltec political control, with the weakening or abandonment of Toltec frontier defenses, and possibly with environmental deterioration as an additional cause of movement, most of these marginal groups would have had little choice but to drift southward into the heart of the former Toltec realm, where they would have constituted a formidable threat to the remaining urban settlements. However, whether they were the agents responsible for the final destruction of the major centers, or whether, instead, primarily internecine warfare among the major centers was involved, remains an open question. The Chichimecs of Xolotl (who clearly were not nomadic food-gatherers but a people long experienced with agriculture), after all, did not themselves overwhelm Tula but arrived there only after the great capital was "fallen and destroyed, its streets overgrown with grass, and totally abandoned" (Dibble 1951: 18).

In calling attention to the complexities of the relationships between the settled political systems, their marginally agricultural outliers, and the seminomadic collectors, Angel Palerm and Eric Wolf rightly stress that the pattern was one involving active acculturation:

Obviously, the adoption of Toltec political, military and agricultural patterns by Chichimecs and marginal farmers involved more than mere imitation. As we have seen, the Toltecs equipped and trained such groups with the purpose of using them as auxiliaries along the frontier and in their internal struggles, as well as settlers. Thus some groups learned agricultural skills, achieved a fairly high level of military organization and efficiency, and came to form tribal federations. When the Toltec order began to weaken, these groups stood ready to penetrate Mesoamerica, to enter into symbiotic relationships with remnant Toltec groups, and in the end to merge with the mainstream of Civilization. This process is exemplified by the Chichimecs of Xolotl, founders of the dynasty which ruled

Texcoco when the Spaniards arrived, and thus founders of one of the most important centers of civilization in Mesoamerica [1957:4].

Here we catch glimpses of the many-layered character of even the major urban centers in prehispanic central Mexico. It closely corresponds to the fluidity of much of the urban population in early Mesopotamia, although differing from the latter in its apparent emphasis on the retention of self-conscious ethnic divisions. How are we to understand the composition of a city like Tula, said to have included not only a Tolteca-Chichimeca elite stratum but also a stratum of Nonoalcas, speaking a different tongue or tongues, venerating different gods, and apparently more skilled in the sedentary arts of construction and craftsmanship? Or the curious amalgam of supposed geographic derivations and separate customs characterizing the groups of specialized craftsmen who were said to preserve the Toltec heritage in the later Aztec capital? Surely even the internal structuring of such cities, to say nothing of the dynamics of their development in relation to their rural hinterlands, requires that we extend beyond the city and its immediately dependent hinterlands and, instead, adopt a regional frame for ecological analysis.

The problem of the relationship between Mesoamerican subsistence patterns and the growth of social differentiation still remains to be adumbrated. There are both striking similarities and important differences between central Mexico and Mesopotamia with respect to systems of cultivation and tenure. While the lands of Aztec commoners (macehuales) were held by corporate kin groups (calpullis) and were inalienable, with hereditable usufruct rights depending on continued cultivation, the conditions of tenure on the lands of the nobility were more fluid. Leaving for a later time discussion of the system of social statuses of which land tenure was only a partial reflection, it is sufficient to note that some estates were hereditable and entailed, reverting to the king in the event of the death of the noble without issue, while others reportedly could be sold or otherwise disposed of. Unfortunately, the sources provide very few details on who the purchasers of land were or under what circumstances purchases were made. All that can be said with certainty is that land was distributed by the king as spoils of war, both to members of noble lineages and to commoners who had distinguished themselves in warfare.

In other words, the available sources from central Mexico attest only the imposition of large-scale landownership "from above," as an act of political largesse accompanying military conquest. The bulk of the population obtained its livelihood only within the framework of corporate kin groups or else as dependent retainers bound to a lord's land and to his service. Under such circumstances the sale of land would appear to be a correspondingly late development, arising only after unentailed fields had accumulated in the hands of the nobility in an unprecedented process of territorial expansion. Indeed, Jacques Soustelle has argued that as late as the time of the arrival of the Spaniards private property was still "in the act of coming into existence" (1962:80). To be sure, we must bear in mind the bias and disproportionate emphasis in most of the contemporary accounts of the powers and activities of royal lineages. Given this narrowly restricted viewpoint in at least the surviving documents, the few passing references to privately held land may assume a greater significance than would otherwise be the case. But it must still be said that on present evidence the role of differential access to land in *generating* class differences remains uncertain.

Generally, it is impossible to determine where privately held lands (i.e., lands not associated with the performance of an office) lay, how significant a proportion of the arable area in different regions they constituted, and whether or not they tended to be devoted to market-oriented production employing more intensive regimes of cultivation. Such information would be particularly important for regions of especially high agricul-

tural productivity and corresponding economic importance, such
as the chinampa regions around the lakes in the Valley of Mexico, but apparently it is as unavailable there as elsewhere. While
the unique but fragmentary "Maguey Map," for example, indicates a rectangular grid of intensively cultivated chinampa-like
houseplots, its position cannot be clearly fixed and it provides
no information on whether the plots represented small-scale
private ownership or merely usufruct rights. Torquemada and
Clavijero describe indigenous maps on which different types
of landholdings were painted in contrasting colors, and late
sixteenth century exemplars of this tradition appear in legal
depositions over Indian rights to land. But, while examples
testifying to prehispanic conditions apparently survived the
initial ravages of the Conquest, they were neither copied nor
preserved for present study.

Although the evidence is admittedly inconclusive, there
are suggestions of a significant, if partial, contrast between
Mesopotamia and central Mexico. In the former, we have seen
that leveling devices involving the redistribution of corporately
held lands apparently were absent, while, on the other hand,
there was vigorous buying and selling not merely among royally appointed officeholders but among small agricultural producers, applying, according to Igor Diakonoff's estimate, to
"at least 40 to 50 per cent of the lands, with about two thirds
of the population" of the important city-state of Lagash at
the end of Early Dynastic times (1954:21). In central Mexico,
on the other hand, the institutions of sale were poorly developed and largely limited to the nobility, while the bulk of
the population enjoyed only a portion of the usufruct (minus
tribute and labor service) of corporately owned, rigorously
entailed land. In the Mesopotamian instance, a contribution
to the growth of social stratification from local differentia in
subsistence seems assured. In Mesoamerica, on the contrary,
the growth of social stratification seems to have been pre-
eminently a politically induced process associated with royal

largesse in the distribution of lands and tribute. Of course, this is not to deny the linkages between politics and subsistence, but at any rate the linkages seem in fundamental respects to have been different ones. Lloyd Fallers provides a succinct statement of what seems an applicable ethnographic parallel:

. . . in traditional Africa goods and services, both as symbols and as facilities, circulate primarily in terms of political relations, for it is the polity that dominates stratification. Persons and groups strive to control the symbols and facilities that are the expressions of authority and the means of strengthening and extending it. A good case could be made that, at least in eastern, central and southern Africa, the most important facilities are people. This does not mean that people are regarded by their rulers as mere "things," though of course various forms of slavery have sometimes been involved, but rather simply that in the production of goods and services in this part of Africa, the most problematic factor is usually human labor.
. . . land is on the whole not scarce and agricultural and military technology are relatively simple. The means of production are therefore controlled by groups of village cultivators. For the chief who wishes to strengthen and extend his rule, the main problem consists in securing an adequate supply of labor. The solution of this problem lies in attracting and holding the maximum number of subjects who, as cultivators and warriors, can then produce the maximum amount of tribute and booty in craft and agricultural products. These in turn can be redistributed as largess to the maximum number of loyal supporters [1964:126].

There is one further respect in which control over productive subsistence resources may have initiated political processes connected with the growth of the state. I refer to Karl Wittfogel's thesis on "Oriental Despotism" (1957). Wittfogel asserts that irrigation-based societies like those commonly associated with the great oriental civilizations constitute a separate class of social phenomena in which a number of interacting institutional features combined to shape a course of development different from what took place among stratified agricultural societies in western Europe. Their special features, he maintains, were the imposition of inordinately strong political controls necessary for hydraulic management, a related tendency for their elites to become monopolistic bureaucracies, close identification of the dominant religion with the officials of the government, and the fractionation and atrophy of private property and other non-state-controlled centers of economic initiative and power. Such societies, after an initial creative period during which they were formed, he regards as stagnating or retrogressing until the impact of modern technical and social changes associated with the Industrial Revolution. One of the areas with which we deal, Mesopotamia, appears in his typology as a "compact" hydraulic society; the central Mexican highlands fall within his "loose" subtype, in which centers of hydraulic agriculture were dispersed rather than concentrated.

I am not concerned here with a general discussion of this grandiose theory, although it may be noted in passing that a detailed scrutiny of the historical development of a number of regions crucial to it tends not to confirm either the specific role of irrigation management in the growth of governmental controls or the existence of structural barriers to further development that Wittfogel adduces. A theory that finds it useful to characterize the temple centers of the Classic lowland Maya as a "marginal hydraulic society" obviously is overdrawn and at least requires radical revision and reduction in scope. But what is important for the present discussion are two empirical questions about the growth of early states in Mesopotamia and central Mexico, which Wittfogel's thesis at least has the virtue of bringing forcefully to our attention. The first concerns the nature of irrigation systems: Were they sufficiently large in scale or complex in managerial requirements *during the periods with which we are dealing* to have served as a stimulus to the growth of specialized political bureaucratic elites? The second concerns the nature of irrigation management, again during our specific periods. Who assumed respon-

sibility for canal construction and maintenance, and how
closely was control over the distribution of water articulated
with other patterns of superordinate authority?

In Mesopotamia there are sporadic references to the construction of occasional large canals and irrigation works in
late Early Dynastic royal inscriptions, but the settled zone
in the main tended to follow bifurcating and rejoining stream
channels running along natural levees. In other words, irrigation, on the whole, was conducted on a small-scale basis,
which involved little alteration of the natural hydraulic regime
and the construction of only relatively small-scale field and
feeder canals that were wholly artificial. To judge from slightly
later times, the allocation of irrigation water was in the hands
of temple officials rather than royally appointed overseers,
and as early as Early Dynastic times the necessary labor forces
for the maintenance work were apparently organized and directed by the individual temples. "In short, there is nothing
to suggest that the rise of dynastic authority in southern
Mesopotamia was linked to the administrative requirements
of a major canal system" (Adams 1960b:281).

Our knowledge of the detailed physical layout of settlements in relation to their irrigated agricultural hinterlands
unfortunately stems almost entirely from the central and
northern parts of the Mesopotamian plain. Here the blanket
of alluvium is very much thicker than around the ancient
Sumerian city-states in the extreme south, and much denser
and more continuous later occupation has also helped to obscure the early patterns. But, pending more intensive reconnaissance in the south, the positioning of settlements around
ancient Eshnunna, in a district east of modern Baghdad, provides the fullest available information:

The main towns . . . do not form the hubs of radiating canal
networks along which the subsidiary villages are strung. . . . The
subsistence requirements for the existing, still comparatively small,
population could have been met with flood irrigation based on tem-

porary dams and small ditches to direct the water, supplemented with, or perhaps increasingly replaced in time by, small canal systems that grew slowly by accretion but that never were extended more than a few kilometers inland from the streams. In the context of Mesopotamian conditions, it has recently been shown that this kind of irrigation is well within the capabilities of local groups without state intervention. Elaborate control works to regulate the water supply certainly were not necessary for so rudimentary an irrigation system. Hence it is difficult to see the emergence of the towns as a consequence of any monopolistic control of the water supply of surrounding villages, and still more difficult to imagine the growth of their political institutions as a consequence of a need for a bureaucracy concerned with canal management [Adams 1965:40–41].

As this description implies, a map of Early Dynastic settlements in Mesopotamia (Fig. 2) tends to convey a false impression about the density and uniformity of ancient land use. In spite of the relatively slight differences in the topography of the alluvial plain between the levees of the braided stream networks that were characteristic of that period and the interior depressions separating them, this system is characterized by decisive ecological boundaries. Much of the land, such as the great Sumerian edin, or pasturing ground, in the empty region between the major southern cities, was permanently unusable for irrigation agriculture within the terms of the political and economic system prevailing until Classical times. The area actually cultivated at any one time was small in relation both to the gross area of potentially arable land and to the amount cultivated during much of the first millennium A.D. and again today. Hence population levels also were relatively low. There is reason to believe that even the largest cities, like Uruk with 450 hectares, were not continuously built up within their walls but included open areas and even cultivated gardens. A maximum urban concentration of fifty thousand persons or so seems consistent with excavated remains and calculations from modern urban densities in the same

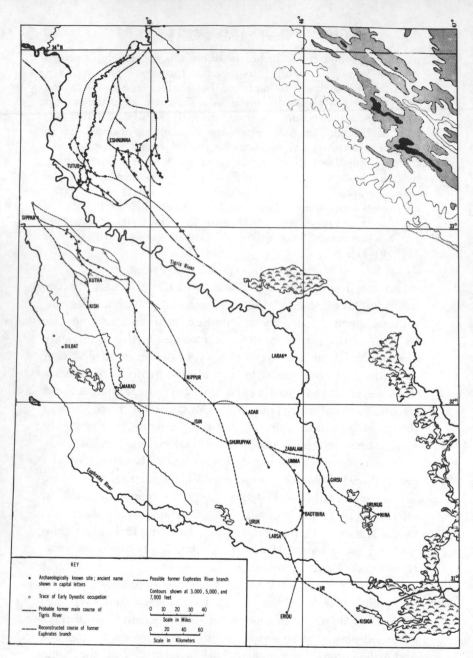

FIGURE 2. Early Dynastic settlements in southern Mesopotamia, and reconstructed network of contemporary watercourses (*After Adams 1958, 1965; Jacobsen 1960; etc.*)

area, and only a handful of Sumerian settlements could have approached even this figure. It follows that a total population for the entire alluvial plain during the first half of the third millennium B.C. of between a half-million and a million persons is perhaps the most reasonable estimate possible with currently available evidence.

As to Mesoamerica, estimates of the population density within the central part of the Aztec realm at the time of the Spanish Conquest vary widely. Systematic and detailed studies by Sherburne F. Cook, Woodrow Borah, and their co-workers,[3] largely based on inferences from tribute rolls in the light of Post-Conquest sources, have been interpreted as suggesting levels significantly higher even than those obtaining under modern conditions of industrialization and rapidly improving public health. According to their estimates, the gross population of central Mexico was on the order of 20 million inhabitants; about 5 million persons would have lived within the heartland of Aztec control shown in Figure 3. Rural densities as high as 800 persons per square kilometer are proposed for the Valley of Mexico, and a correspondingly high estimate of 360,000 persons is given for the population of the Tenochtitlán-Tlatelolco urban cluster.

Some of the assumptions underlying these estimates are clearly debatable, and a recent review of the Old World evidence by R. J. Russell (1958) seems to indicate that they are excessively high in comparison not only with Mesopotamia but with preindustrial societies generally. Quite possibly Mexico attained population levels substantially higher than those of early Mesopotamia, in spite of the close similarities in the Urban Revolutions that transformed both areas. But it is difficult to believe that the two areas could differ, as the Cook and Borah figures imply, by a full order of magnitude. And, in any case, just as in Mesopotamia, it is impossible to support

3. Most recently, Borah and Cook 1963. A full bibliography of earlier works is included therein.

an explanation of Aztec militarism and expansionism in terms
of increasing demographic pressure as a major independent
variable. As Pedro Armillas observes,

This *Lebensraum* justification fails to explain the facts. Undoubtedly, the high density of occupation on the central plateau provided
stimulus and manpower for aggression. Nevertheless, the purpose
of resettling populations is never mentioned as a motive for waging
war in the native chronicles, nor did the conquests result in large-
scale movements of people, although in some instances military
colonists were established in newly conquered marches to defend
the frontier [1964b:323–24].

In light of the possibility of greater population densities
in Mesoamerica than in Mesopotamia, the problem of Mesoamerican irrigation is of particular interest. At present, however, a summary evaluation of the role of prehispanic irrigation
is more difficult, since important new data on the problem is
continuing to be brought forward. An intensive study of documentary sources by Angel Palerm has disclosed references to
almost 400 widely scattered instances of irrigation in late prehispanic times, their distribution perhaps implying, as he suggests, "a considerable antiquity." In most cases the systems
were of no more than local importance, but the largest works,
and the greatest concentration of references to them, "coincide,
in general terms, with the greatest densities of population,
with the distribution of the most important urban centers and
with the nuclei of political power and military expansion"
(1954:71). Clearly, techniques of irrigation agriculture played
a not insignificant part in Mesoamerican subsistence patterns
of at least the late prehispanic period.

Our special concern here, however, is not with the importance of irrigation as one of the vital, interacting factors increasing agricultural productivity and hence surpluses, or even
with its possible contribution to the growth of social stratification through its encouragement of differential yields. If perhaps
not quite to the same degree, these effects of irrigation almost

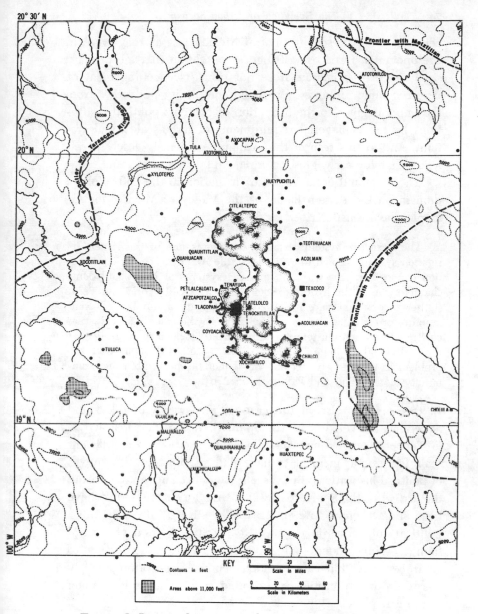

FIGURE 3. Late prehispanic settlements in central Mexico, largely from Aztec documentary sources. (*After Barlow 1949.*)

certainly were present in central Mexico just as they were in Mesopotamia. But it is Wittfogel's contention that the primary significance of irrigation arose not from its encouragement of new economic resources and social complexity but rather from the impetus given to the formation of coercive political institutions by the managerial requirements of large-scale canal systems. And in this respect the available evidence, closely paralleling that for early Mesopotamia, fails to support him.

The scale and organization of irrigation in the Old Acolhua domain on the eastern flanks of the Valley of Mexico, for example, has been described as follows:

> The Texcocan system certainly represents one of the largest irrigation systems known to date in Middle America. Yet its construction cannot compare with the massive systems of dykes and dams characteristic of the hydraulic societies of the Old World and Peru. Rather modest in scale, it served to integrate a number of communities or settlement areas into what might be called an "irrigation cluster." . . . Such clusters . . . differ from "local irrigation" in that the individual community lacks direct access to water, and the problem of allocating water can no longer be met within one community alone [Wolf and Palerm 1955:276].

In this case, as also in the case of the system of dikes and aqueducts marveled at by the Spaniards upon their first arrival in Tenochtitlán, we may indeed have irrigation on a sufficient scale for its management to have had an effect on the growth of political institutions. But these systems are known to antedate the arrival of the Spaniards by less than a century and to have been undertaken as state enterprises by strong, fully constituted political authorities in response to a critical period of general famine. While undoubtedly they may have served further to centralize and intensify political controls, accordingly they were hardly responsible for bringing such controls into being in the first place.

A perhaps more significant, but also more ambiguous, case concerns the valley of Teotihuacán to the north of Texcoco and the extraordinary urban center that flourished there a full millennium and more before the Texcocan irrigation system. This is not the point at which to discuss Teotihuacán itself, except to indicate that René Millon's surveys confront us with the hitherto unimagined problem of an enormous ceremonial and population cluster covering close to thirty square kilometers early in the first millennium A.D., several times the largest estimates (already mystifyingly large) of less than a decade ago. What is important in the present context, however, is the subsistence pattern that sustained this great urban center, and here the arguments for its dependence upon irrigation that have been put forward by William Sanders, although admittedly all based upon indirect evidence like the placement of contemporary outlying sites with relation to springs, channeled watercourses, and alluvial fans, seem cumulatively conclusive (n.d., pp. 73-74).

Having admitted the presence of irrigation at Teotihuacán, however, we must concede that we have "explained" very little. The springs provide irrigation water only for an area of some 38 square kilometers, an area not substantially larger than the urban zone alone and in terms of size surely to be classified as no more than an irrigation "cluster" or "district" in Wolf's and Palerm's terms. That such an incredible concentration of urban growth should coincide with a relatively modest irrigation system, of a type that elsewhere can both come into being and be sustained merely as a result of informal, ad hoc arrangements between villagers, merely underlines the limited role that irrigation management must have played. Its complex system of hierarchies, after all, surely exercised administrative control over a very large surrounding—largely unirrigated—region.

Not unreasonably, Sanders believes that, if irrigation helped to provide the subsistence base on which Teotihuacán was built, the introduction of irrigation techniques ought to be traced back to the period of its first explosive transformation into an urban center, the Proto-Classic at about the beginning of the Christian Era. Direct corroboration is still lacking, but it may be significant that objects of the same date recently have been reported to occur in the silts of the intensively cultivated chinampa district near Xochimilco. It is interesting to note that in both cases the initial efforts were probably directed in the main toward the reclamation of swampy land through drainage, a characteristically simpler undertaking than canal irrigation with scarce and erratic water supplies and one fully consistent with small-scale local initiative and an absence of superordinate political control. Yet the possibility that canal irrigation may have been present at an even earlier time is raised by preliminary reports of reconnaisance findings in the Tehuacán valley of southeastern Puebla. It would be a foolhardy archeologist who would insist that no further surprises of this kind are in store for us.

As befits the diversity of the Mesoamerican terrain and the rapid pace of current research there, any summary statement on the role of irrigation management in the formation of prehispanic states has apodictic overtones that must be explicitly denied. The conclusion does seem warranted, however, that irrigation even on the limited scale of early Mesopotamia, binding together at most a small handful of communities and perhaps helping to consolidate coersive political controls but not requiring them, was widely scattered, dwarfed by the scale of the polities accompanying it, and generally late in making an appearance. No more than in Mesopotamia, then, and in all probability less, can we look to the managerial requirements of irrigation as the major stimulus to the growth of the institutions of the state. In both areas irrigation merely forms a subsidiary part of a functionally interdependent network of subsistence techniques, political hierarchies, and economic relationships. And our task of understanding this network will not be advanced by isolating irrigation as the primary, independent causative agency.

The physical manifestations of urban settlement in Mesopotamia and central Mexico are less central to our theme than the ecological setting in which they arose and, in any case, were too complex and extensive to receive detailed discussion. The end products in both areas were true cities, hundreds (in the case of Teotihuacán, thousands) of hectares of densely built-up agglomeration of architectural components, secular and ceremonial, public and private, planned and unplanned. For central Mexico, our near-total ignorance of the archeological aspects of the more important late prehispanic towns is more than offset both by depictions of palaces and temples in surviving codices and by the luminous impressions left by such of the Conquistadores as Bernal Díaz, the Anonymous Conqueror, and Hernán Cortés himself.

Although less adequate for the Akkadian period than for the Early Dynastic period, on the whole the archeological record for Mesopotamia is relatively good. We can plot the limits of a half-dozen or more major towns with considerable assurance; we have detailed knowledge of several palaces, of numerous temples, and of a large, if perhaps not fully representative, array of private houses. In at least a few cases, notably in the district around ancient Eshnunna in the northern part of the alluvial plain, not only can the full sequence of construction of these types of structures be traced individually, but also the extent of excavations is sufficient for a sense of their spatial distribution in relation to one another to be obtained as well. But we have no sources comparable to the Spanish accounts on which we rely so heavily for Mesoamerica, sources which, for all their impressionism and imprecision, alone can invest dead floor plans with people, ceremonies, a widely extended web of social interrelations, and the ebb and flow of day-to-day life.

Given these fundamental differences and the bifurcation in the nature of our sources, a detailed comparison of urban layouts and their architectural components in Mesopotamia and Mesoamerica would be a largely futile exercise. It would also be a misleading and unnecessary one. It is the institutions of city life as they emerged and interacted with one another that constitute the appropriate units of study for comparative purposes. The towns and cities that came into being in both areas were no more than the gross outer manifestations of the totality of this process, the containers, in the apt phrase of Lewis Mumford (1960:7), within which it took place.

III

KIN AND CLASS

ALMOST BY DEFINITION, THE GROWTH OF SOCIAL COMPLEXITY HAS been accompanied by social stratification. If the term "class" is used to describe objectively differentiated degrees of access to the means of production of the society without any necessary implications of sharply reduced mobility, class consciousness, or overt interclass struggle, the early states characteristically were class societies. Hence perhaps the central task in a comparative essay is to consider parallelisms both in emergent class structures and in the sequence of changes by which they were brought about.

This is a task to which Lewis Henry Morgan first gave concrete historical embodiment. Perhaps deriving some of his ideas from Sir Henry Maine, he formulated the development of the state in terms of the failure of gentile institutions to meet the increasingly complex needs of society. These needs he associatd, first, with the presence of agriculture and, second, with the rise of cities:

. . . in the Upper Status [of barbarism], cities surrounded with ring embankments, and finally with walls of dressed stone, appear for the first time in human experience. Cities of this grade imply the existence of a stable and developed field agriculture, the possession of domestic animals in flocks and herds, of merchandise in masses and of property in houses and lands. The city brought with it new demands in the art of government by creating a changed condition of society [1963:264].

Today, with knowledge of a long line of antecedents of both

Old and New World civilizations of which Morgan knew nothing, this general view still commands respect. Most students
would shift the emphasis from property as such, socially defined and maintained rights to certain resources or commodities,
to the system of stratified social relations of which rights to
property were only an expression. Probably most would also
tend to question Morgan's implicit assumption that the substitution of territorially defined communities for ethnically defined
ones was both a necessary and a sufficient cause for the growth
of the institution of private property. But there can be little
dissent with the general shift he posited from ascriptively defined groupings of persons to politically organized units based
on residence. And, substituting class stratification for property,
I, for one, still share his conviction that it was the "mainspring"
and "foundation" of political society (p. 224).

Hence we must undertake a comparison of the nature of social stratification in early Mesopotamia and central Mexico,
with reference both to the processes by which it emerged and
to the forms it ultimately assumed. Obviously, it is easier to
describe the latter than to trace the former. There are important
differences between Spanish sources that recount Aztec jural
rules and behavior patterns (usually not differentiating these
two aspects of a social system), on the one hand, and cuneiform
sources that for the most part fail to indicate either the jural or
institutional setting of the narrowly focused relationships they
record, on the other. But in both cases the description of the
fully developed systems can be based on a relative abundance
of material. For earlier periods, by contrast, we can rely only
on records that are substantially less well understood and reliable, and ultimately on the data of archeology alone.

Accordingly, it is useful to reverse the historical sequence
for the present and begin with a necessarily brief and somewhat
overgeneralized comparison of the relationship between kin-
based patterns of organization and stratified social groupings
in the two areas at their latest point. This procedure has the

added virtue of adumbrating some of the basic similarities in structure between late Early Dynastic–Akkadian Mesopotamia, on the one hand, and late prehispanic central Mexico, on the other. On this basis we can then turn more easily to the vital questions of the similarities in processes of growth, which it is my main purpose to elicit.

As we turn first to Mesopotamia, a cautionary word is necessary. Sumerologists only recently have begun to turn their attention to social and economic questions after a period of many years in which the existence of a so-called *Tempelwirtschaft* was taken for granted on the basis of the pioneering but somewhat misconstrued and overgeneralized work of Father Anton Deimel on archives from ancient Shurppak and Lagash (cf. Schneider 1920; Deimel 1931). Even without consideration of the massive philological problems confronting students of these documents, there are important unanswered questions about their representativeness and about the proper methodology for their interpretation. The entire body of material needs interdisciplinary, quantitively oriented restudy, as well as systematic comparison with the contemporary archeological data, with indirect suggestions as to socioeconomic organization provided by historical and literary texts, and with more fragmentary documentary sources for the same period from other sites.

Provisionally, pending the completion of restudies now under way, we may begin by noting that Sumerian referential kin terminology (terms of address occur rarely, and only in formal literary contexts) follows generational lines. Terms for "cousin" and "aunt" seemingly are absent, but "father's brother" is recognized,[1] possibly indicating a preferential marriage pattern that is not explicitly attested in the documentary sources because of their limited, largely administrative subject matter. In particular, the wide geographical spread and considerable known time depth of patrilateral parallel cousin marriage among

---

1. Ake Sjøberg, personal communication.

the Bedouin and many groups of settled Arab peasantry may suggest that it is a pattern of immense durability, which already existed in Sumerian times. Robert Murphy and Leonard Kasdan (1959:27-28) have argued plausibly that it lends a quality of "resilience and adaptability in the face of adversity" while still permitting the periodic formation of great tribal coalitions that are vertically integrated through genealogical reckoning to common ancestors. But, though these important functional and ecological advantages lend plausibility to a suggestion of continuity, the presence of a well-developed system of Sumerian affinal terminology differentiates between the ancient and the present systems. Hence many aspects of the character of the former, including the underlying question of whether or not the agnatic sections constituting the central components of the structure were mainly endogamous or exogamous, still remain obscure.

Marriage, in any case, was prevailingly—and perhaps exclusively, except for the royal court—monogamous. To judge from records of land sale and from historical inscriptions (both perhaps unrepresentative in that they focus primarily on members of the elite), descent was reckoned in the male line. Cases are known, on the other hand, in which genealogies also include individual women among those through whom descent is traced. Moreover, women occasionally appear in land deeds and on ration lists as heads of households (perhaps widows) and as both the donors and recipients of ritualized food offerings. Furthermore, cases are known in which women carried on long-distance trade in their own names and filled important administrative posts beside their husbands, for example, Baranamtarra, the wife of the ruler Lugalanda in late Early Dynastic Lagash. To judge from ration lists, records of inheritance, and the architectural plans of contemporary private houses, the customary urban residential unit was the nuclear family.

Traces of larger, more inclusive organizations can be discerned that mediated certain relationships between individuals or families, on the one hand, and the institutions of the state, on the other, although they are only occasionally and ambiguously referred to in the specialized archives upon which we must rely. It is only reasonable to assume that their importance in the informal, almost wholly unrecorded day-to-day life of the community was much greater than such references alone would suggest. At least some of these groups seemingly were localized and corporately held title to agricultural lands. Administrative references to others suggest that they were primarily of an occupational or professional character, although perhaps also localized in places of residence and employment. The latter bear comparison with guilds, in that their recruitment and internal structure must have followed kin lines; moreover, they acted as corporate bodies in the fulfillment of certain "external" civic responsibilities.

We are indebted for the primary studies on corporate landholding groups to Igor Diakonoff (1954), who has been the first to explain satisfactorily a number of enigmatic deeds of sale and other records connected with the transfer of land in Early Dynastic times. Most of these documents, stemming from Sippar, Adab, Eshnunna, Shuruppak, Lagash, and other widely scattered localities, had long been known, but their significance did not become apparent until they were studied as a group. Now it appears that among these documents— Diakonoff recognizes 35 or so that are of Early Dynastic date— are a number recording purchases in which there are multiple sellers in a corporate, although by no means equal, relation to one another. Commonly, one or a few individuals are listed as "owners" of a field or at least as recipients (literally, "eaters") of its price in barley, silver, or other commodities. But also included are references to "sons of the field" (this category sometimes including women!), "brothers of the owners of the field," and others who seemingly give assent to the sale by their presence and who generally receive in return a gift of bread, fish, milk, etc. Diakonoff notes that the actual ritual of transfer is carried out in the name of the corporate group as a whole, the "house of . . . ," rather than that of the "owners," while in one particularly revealing case the "owners" are further characterized as "men elected by the house of. . . ." Incidentally, the numbers of individuals involved in these transactions can be relatively large; in one example that dates from the Akkadian period 600 men of Marad were feasted by Manishtusu for two days in connection with a purchase of land.

Unfortunately, such restricted and laconic notations of sale (particularly since they were recorded from the point of view of the purchaser) can give us very little insight into the internal structure and authority systems of the corporate groups who were the sellers. The fact that a considerable number of texts are known which record the sale of small, privately held subsistence plots strongly suggests that even outside the ambit of the great state institutions the organization of the agricultural population into kin-oriented groupings was incomplete. Moreover, the documents Diakonoff has collected betray substantial differences in at least the formal relationships between the "owners" or principal representatives and their followers. All the foregoing hints at an institution that probably varied locally in form and importance, nowhere represented the exclusive mode of community organization, and was more or less rapidly being eroded away by changing social conditions such as the concentration of landholdings. This theme will be returned to presently.

Among the archives of the state institutions and private estates in Lagash and elsewhere there are references of a different sort to units, implicitly based, at least in part, on kin affiliations, into which their male constituents were grouped. For certain purposes, particularly in connection with personnel lists specifying the distribution of rations, the affiliation of individuals with these larger units on the apparent basis of descent is carefully specified. The absence of references to landholdings in these instances may, of course, be only a reflection of the special purposes of the documents rather than of the characteristics of the groups themselves. On the other hand, while many of the groups are named after animals (snakes, donkeys, etc.) or gods (*lú-ᵈENKI*), a number of others are descriptively entitled with the names of professions (silversmiths, carpenters, leatherworkers, heralds, etc.) (Gelb 1957:251-52). Perhaps these groups can be collectively entitled im-ru-a, lineages or clans, whether composed of craftsmen or agriculturists. As early as the time of the Shuruppak documents (near the beginning of Early Dynastic III) we hear of 539 dumu-dumu grouped in seven im-ru, with the functions of each servant in the palace being assigned on the basis of his lineage. In the time of Gudea, about 2200 B.C., we find that energetic ruler of Lagash calling up his population behind the emblems of their im-ru-a to perform specialized services in connection with the rebuilding of the temple of Ningirsu.

Having recognized the existence of lineage or clan modes of organization, not only in landholding but also in craft and professional groupings, it is not unreasonable to suppose that kin affiliation played an important role even in many cases where it is not attested in what are, after all, mainly highly condensed compilations for administrative purposes. For example, in the militias of the Early Dynastic city-states, craftsmen and other occupational specialists were mustered in platoons under their regular foremen, with platoons in turn formed into companies under the leadership of palace officials. Now, while there is no evidence that the units were composed of individuals related by descent or that their leadership was internally sanctioned rather than superimposed as a stratum of minor officials, it must be remembered that what was important to the muster-roll clerks was not the degree of internal kin affiliation characterizing these units but their specialized functions and their cohesiveness for military purposes. Hence the absence of such evidence means virtually nothing. It would have been only natural for the palace to treat the heads of these groups as administratively defined "foremen," with 50 per cent higher rations than their crews, rather than as ascriptively defined "headmen." But, again, it is simply not shown that they were so regarded internally.

How far are we justified in reconstructing a system of kin organization from such ambiguous and fragmentary evidence? The specialized Sumerologist has the responsibility of remaining close to his sources. The task of the comparatively oriented anthropologist, on the other hand, is to place them in a more generalized framework—taking for granted that the framework will involve interpretive errors but also taking for granted that the cumulative advance of his field depends upon the generation of testable hypotheses and their progressive refinement. In these terms, it is not the lacunae in the data but their consistency that is most impressive. Clearly, there were groupings of nuclear families into ascriptive units organized at least in part along lines of descent. Such groups in some (and perhaps in most) cases corporately held title to agricultural lands. They also played a role in the organization of the crafts, of corvée labor called up by the state for certain purposes, and probably of the army. Such widely manifested functions suggest that lineage groupings had not become merely vestigial by late Early Dynastic and Akkadian times but, instead, were still both powerful and important. The absence of more numerous references to them is fully and satisfactorily explained by the particular, limited purposes for which the existing texts were recorded.

Turning to central Mexico, we find ramifying organizations based on both kinship and residence that were essentially similar to what has been traced in Mesopotamia. Given the nature of our sources in this case, there is no difficulty in establishing at least the basic structure and activities of the more inclusive units, the so-called "calpullis." Although the complexities of their changing relationship to the primary institutions of the state remain in dispute and although there are fewer possibilities for quantitative studies than in Mesopotamia, the Spanish accounts have the inestimable virtue of having quite naturally described calpullis as part of the warp and woof of the entire institutional setting.

The bulk of the commoner population, at least in towns whose lands had not been appropriated by conquest, seem to have resided in nuclear family units. While polygyny was present, the available references to it are very largely restricted to the nobility—for whom Friedrich Katz (1956:122) argues that it created the special problem of a disproportionate population increase in their class. The status of women apparently was in decline at the time of the Conquest but yet remained relatively high in that rights to inherit land and to exercise certain professions were still retained. In this respect, as in many others, close parallels with late Early Dynastic and Akkadian Mesopotamia are obvious.

As in Mesopotamia, our primary interest centers on the more inclusive units into which such households were grouped. While debate continues over the precise nature of the calpullis, the trend of all more recent research supports the conclusion that they were localized endogamous lineages that under most circumstances maintained their own lands and temples and that, particularly in urbanized, politically organized communities, also exercised a variety of other functions. Even the Spaniards were not entirely consistent in their translation of the word. Usually they spoke of calpullis as "barrios" or quarters, emphasizing the aspect of these groups as zones of contiguous residence. But on other occasions they spoke of them as "lineages" and defined their leaders as "elder kinsmen." In fact, Zurita, one of the most penetrating of early Spanish observers, often translates the term by both words together. In any event, officers were chosen by election from the group, although generally from the same family.

Lands corporately owned by the calpullis were apportioned

both for the house plots of their members and for cultivation by the individual families. In the event that cultivation was not continued or families moved away, the plots reverted to the officers of the calpulli, who either reassigned them to new families without lands or directed their cultivation in common to maintain tribute quotas or for similar purposes. Except under these circumstances, however, there is good evidence that redistributive mechanisms were not systematically applied for the purpose of equalizing wealth within the group. Gross variation is reported—by a factor of ten or more even within single communities—in the size of calpulli lands allocated to individual families. Moreover, some calpulli members either had somehow lost their holdings or had always lacked land entirely, occasionally being forced into slavery or emigration as a result. The source of these differences is not clear, since lands could not be sold by calpulli members holding usufruct rights to them. Still, as M. Acosta Saignes (1945:16) has noted, there are occasional reports of the sale of land with the approval of calpulli officers, as well as of land being privately owned by merchants, which must indicate that land could be alienated by corporate action under some circumstances.

Alluding to their fluid combination of features of both class and clan, Eric Wolf has persuasively called attention to the resemblance between calpullis and what have been called

"conical clans," kinship units which bind their members with common familial ties but which distribute wealth, social standing, and power most unequally among the members of the pseudo-family. Such kin units trace their descent back to an original ancestor, real or fictitious; but, at the same time, they regularly favor his lineal descendants over the junior or 'cadet' lines in regulating access to social, economic, or political prerogatives [1959:136].

If the paradigm applies to calpullis, it may also apply to the Sumerian im-ru-a, although in the latter case no evidence is available on whether or not the group was endogamous. And what is even more interesting is that the resemblances between these two concrete instances do not stop with their stratified internal arrangements but go on to include many of their relationships with other institutions in their respective societies as well.

Consider some of the other features and activities of calpullis. They served with their own emblems and leadership as the core of the Aztec armies under the control of officers appointed by the palace. Such was the case also in the early Sumerian city-states. As a closely related feature, not attested in the Sumerian instance but possibly only absent because of the particular limitations of the cuneiform sources, the calpullis also assumed responsibility for the training of their young men for war in a special establishment maintained for that purpose. Directly comparable to the situation that has been described in ancient Sumer, calpullis frequently specialized in certain crafts and professions, providing a characteristic "guild"-like aspect to craft production. Ixtlilxochitl speaks, for example, of the more than thirty crafts practiced by the inhabitants of Tenochtitlán, each with its own quarter—a view whose exclusiveness, to be sure, is challenged by the testimony of other authorities. Unfortunately, there is no direct testimony on what proportion of these specialized members of calpullis also maintained subsistence plots and thus were at least part-time farmers as well. However, one indication that most of them were essentially full-time specialists comes from descriptions by the Conquistadores of the extraordinary *daily* markets in great centers like Tlatelolco. Moreover, at least in the case of craftsmen employed on behalf of the royal court, they were supplied with slaves to meet their subsistence needs or were directly provisioned from the royal stores of tribute. If the inference that regular participation in the market was the general rule not only for merchants but also for craftsmen is correct, then in this respect, as with respect to market activities generally, there was at least a formal difference from the practice in early Mesopotamia.

The calpullis were, we may assume, a traditional means of organizing social relationships, with particular reference to subsistence resources, residence, and profession, a means which long antedated not only the arrival of the Aztecs in central Mexico but probably their Chichimec and Toltec predecessors as well. Possibly they are already implied by the numerous enclosed "palace" compounds that are known at Teotihuacán, each seemingly composed of several private apartments opening on a central court. Moreover, it is interesting to note that there are suggestions at Teotihuacán of localized concentrations of obsidian and pottery wastes within that "Classic" period city, suggesting that the congruence of craft production with kin and residential units may have emerged as the prevailing pattern by that time.

Since our central concern is the growth of the state, the diversification and stratification within calpullis is perhaps of less interest than the ways in which they were articulated with the growing needs of the political institutions characterizing the Aztec realm. Service in the army, already mentioned, is among these articulations. Given the particular pattern of expansion that the Aztecs maintained—an essentially predatory process involving the forced exaction of tribute from conquered towns with few compensating benefits from pacification, improved administration, or even capital improvements designed to enhance the tributary base—the strength and cohesiveness of the army obviously was vital. As the economy of the capital came to be supported increasingly—some even argue primarily —by receipts of tribute from subjugated enemies, the military duties of the calpulli, at least in the eyes of the state, undoubtedly began to overshadow their purely productive functions. But, before the expansion of the realm began to provide external sources of tribute, the institutions of the state depended very largely on "internal" surpluses made available through the calpulli system itself.

The intricacies of this internal tributary system, as well as differences between the interpretations of various authorities, need not concern us. The basic features of the system, at a level of generality suitable for comparison with Mesopotamia, were identical whether applied to calpulli or to subject towns; hence Zurita's succinct description of the system as it applied to the latter can serve for the former also:

> Tribute commonly was paid in maize, peppers, beans and cotton, and fields were designated for this purpose by each town. The rulers kept a number of slaves, who guarded and cultivated these fields with the aid of the townspeople. People whose towns did not have tributary lands set aside also came and assisted in this task, but otherwise they cultivated their own lands and did not travel elsewhere. Firewood, water, and household service also were given to the lords as tribute. Craftsmen gave tribute in that which was their specialty. Tribute was never apportioned by heads, but instead each town and craft was told what it must give and then assigned this amount among its members and brought it at the appointed time.
>
> Tribute was not paid according to the value of either fields or estates, but in crops and other products. All was produced by communal labor, save the tribute of the craftsmen, fishermen, hunters, and those who gave fruit and pottery [1941:146, 152].

In essence, then, this is a system based on labor service, although in urban groups not directly engaged in agriculture the labor may have found its major expression in the production of commodities. Its characteristic form was the setting-aside of fields within local communities for the cultivation of which those communities were collectively responsible and whose entire harvest was to be delivered to the state. Obviously, the need for central accounting was at a minimum under the system, and the apparatus of direct state control did not extend further into the body politic than the traditional leaders or representatives of the local communities. And the latter, as we have seen, continued to be defined on the basis not only of localized residence and corporate control of land but also of real or fictive kinship.

Assuming that these basic, most widespread elements comprised the antecedent form of the tribute system, the great expansion of the Aztec realm in the fifteenth century led to its partial modification. As a result of the appearance of new administrative problems of unprecedented complexity, a specialized group of officials (if hardly a bureaucracy in the fully developed sense) were appointed and charged with the collection of tribute. At least in the surviving documentary evidence, only then do we find the beginnings of a trend toward supplementing the demand for labor service on lands reserved for that purpose with a demand for specified quantities of foodstuffs, raw materials, or locally manufactured products. But, even with this apparent innovation, insofar as the state was concerned, the lowest level of responsibility recognized for furnishing tribute was not the individual citizen but the local community and its representatives as a corporate body.

It is important to note that labor service, whether in tribute, in building, or in personal attendance upon members of the political and religious elites, did not represent an innovation but merely an extension of the existing practice within calpullis. The testimony of Zurita again will serve as an illustration:

The calpullec were a numerous group, and comprised almost all of those who paid tribute to the supreme ruler. Each calpulli also cultivated a field for the sustenance of its principal or head, and gave him service in proportion to the number of people in the ward. This was in recompense for the care he took of them, and for his expenditure on the annual meeting held in his house in support of the general welfare. Tribute to the calpulli head was not paid upon command of the supreme lord, nor as an obligation, but because it was regarded as their most ancient custom. This was independent of the tribute paid to the supreme ruler [p. 142].

Two further, seemingly contradictory, points remain to be made about the effects of the Mexican tribute system on the relationships between the state institutions and the substratum of calpullis. The first is that, at least for the cities forming the Triple Alliance, whose population were the beneficiaries of redistributed tribute collected from the increasingly large number of subjugated towns, the system in time must have tended to corrode the internal autonomy and cohesiveness of the calpullis and to generate new patterns of organization and new loyalties directly linking the population with the state. For example, the state itself undertook the distribution to the populace of the tribute it had received in excess of its other requirements, the state provided gifts of commodities and land to its victorious soldiery, the state assumed the responsibility for meeting the needs of the poor from its own reserves, and the state underwrote the costs of many festivals. Moreover, the availability of redistributed tribute surely must have increased the stratification within calpullis to some extent, and the increasing emphasis on military activities would have tended to bring forward patterns of organization in which the traditional leadership of calpullis could play only a very subordinate role. Thus the sharp division between political patterns of organization at the upper levels and solidary kin communities comprising the great bulk of the population at the lower levels must have tended to blur and disappear more or less rapidly during the final decades of Aztec rule.

The opposing, or at any rate qualifying, point is that the extent and rapidity of this process of "politicization" should not be overdrawn. It would have taken place mainly in the handful of major urban centers with substantial tribute to redistribute, and even there the basic loyalties of the population, like by far the greater part of their day-to-day activities, must have continued to be framed in terms of traditional alliances of kinship and residence. Elsewhere, as the extraordinary durability of "closed corporate" communities throughout Middle America after the Conquest suggests, the effects of newly imposed patterns of political control must have been relatively slight and certainly transient. Bandelier's and Morgan's view that Aztec organization remained only "social" and not "political," that at best it was a military democracy founded upon gentile institutions (Morgan 1963:220), on the whole has been set aside by more recent students as a distortion of the evidence. But, while those early writers failed to perceive the dynamism and significance of some newly emergent Aztec institutions, their characterization is perhaps still very close to the realities of everyday life for all but a very small elite.

Thus we find that traditional, localized groupings, composed of related nuclear families, were the elementary units upon which the states of Early Dynastic Mesopotamia and late prehispanic central Mexico were erected. These units in both cases seem to have taken the form of "conical clans," in which the degree of relationship to a real or fictive common ancestor served as a basis for internal tendencies toward stratification. Probably they were of high antiquity, considerably antedating the onset of civilized life by any definition, and there seems no reason to question Paul Kirchoff's assertion that they represented "the *condition sine qua non*" for the formation of complex, flexible hierarchies of economic and social differentiation that characterized the growth of the state itself (1959:268). At the same time, however, they survived the superimposition of new political relationships for a considerable time, retaining loyalties and forms of internal organization that were rooted in kin relationships, while adapting to the needs of the state through the elaboration of a new series of specialized functions. Among the specialized functions, three in particular may be mentioned: (1) serving as units for military training and service; (2) providing a corporate framework for the development, employment, and retention of the skills and attitudes of specialized craftsmanship; and (3) serving as units of labor management for state projects and services.

Turning from cohesive bonds based on real or fictive kin affiliations within social segments, we must consider the growth of differentiated, hierarchical principles of organization affecting the society at large. What is our evidence for the development of social stratification? What forms did it take in our respective areas? Can we identify a common structure of stratification beneath the welter of divergent local features? Of course, this problem is complicated by the fact that we are dealing with relatively "primitive," undifferentiated systems in which social stratification did not develop as an autonomous, distinctive feature but was "embedded" in multifunctional institutions embracing political and religious components as well. But I believe it remains a valid analytical entity, and without such entities essays in comparison like this one could consist only of contrasting social systems as descriptively integrated wholes—and hence would be foredoomed.

To begin with early Mesopotamia, the available evidence takes a succession of forms which influence the interpretations that can be made of it. In the late Ubaid period, apparently the "take-off" point for the Urban Revolution, it consists almost exclusively of reports from excavations in cemeteries, for example, more than two hundred graves excavated at Eridu, as well as others at Ur and al-Ubaid. Differentiation in grave wealth cannot necessarily be linked directly to differences in status, at least in the absence of converging lines of inference from other evidence. It is therefore fortunate that the broad trend toward increasing differentiation disclosed by later graves from Khafajah, Kish, Jemdet Nasr, Shuruppak, and, above all, Ur can be at first supplemented and confirmed, and ultimately overshadowed, by textual and archeological evidence on aspects of social differentiation other than those associated with mortuary practices.

In the late Ubaid period significant differentiation in grave wealth was almost entirely absent. Normal grave furniture consisted of one or more pottery vessels placed near the feet, with, in some cases, the substitution of stone vessels for those of clay and the occasional addition of pottery figurines and of decorative bands of beads on the clothing of the deceased. In the

Warka and Protoliterate periods greater variation begins to be apparent. Stone maceheads, a copper spear-point, and greater numbers of stone vessels are attested. About one-third of the 25 graves beneath the floors of late Protoliterate private houses at Khafajah were accompanied by stone bowls, and two contained somewhat larger (although still modest) accumulations, including a few well-made vessels of copper, lead, and stone, as well as the usual pottery.

A much larger number of graves of roughly Protoliterate date have been excavated at Ur, although unfortunately the chronological placement of many of them is somewhat doubtful. Of the 340 or so that have been described, less than 10 per cent contain only pottery, while 61 contain one or two simple lead cups or other metal objects. Only two graves of this large series suggest substantial concentrations of wealth, and in both cases the accompanying pottery implies a somewhat later date than the excavator attributes to them. Both contain beads and ornaments of carnelian and lapis lazuli, a few copper and lead bowls and other utensils, considerable numbers of stone vessels, and, of course, pottery. On the assumption that they may be assigned only to the very end of the Protoliterate period at the earliest, they suggest the beginnings of a trend toward increasing differentiation but certainly do not indicate that processes of social stratification had as yet proceeded very far.

With the advent of writing and representational art in the Protoliterate period, the picture can be somewhat sharpened and amplified. Signs already appear for "slave girl" among the earliest Protoliterate tablets, while that for "male slave" seemingly occurs slightly later. The term for "slave" is a derivative from an expression for "foreign country," perhaps suggesting that the institution originated either in the taking of war captives or in the impressment of seminomadic groups who drifted into the settlements after their herds fell below an acceptable minimum for subsistence. Bound "war captives" apparently are shown on a celebrated seal impression from Uruk, although it may be significant that male slaves appear not only later but also in far smaller numbers than do female ones. Possibly the means for the retention and effective employment of male captives had not yet been worked out, so that they were generally killed. Unfortunately, the functional basis for the institution of slavery at the time cannot be determined from the poorly understood texts. Nor are we justified in uncritically inferring that the complex, fully crystallized patterns of the late Early Dynastic period were already present merely on the basis of the occurrence of the terms.

Other contemporary gradations of status are even less clear. There are imposing representations of priests and "king"-like figures, but in general they create more questions than they answer: What portion of the conceptual continuum between mythopoeic thought and "reality" do they portray? Do they illustrate "events" or rituals? And, if mainly rituals, as seems likely, do the apparent importance and specialized roles of individuals within that context necessarily reflect their general status as well? At any event, since we must postpone the discussion of specific political and religious functions until the following chapter, it can be noted here only that representational art possibly does reflect some of the attributes and activities of new elites that would not be known from the available reports of cemeteries in spite of the fairly large number of graves that have been excavated.

As a perhaps significant bit of negative evidence, it may be noted that the terms lu, "full, free citizen," and mash-en-kak, perhaps "commoner of subordinate status," other major components of Mesopotamian society in historic times, do not occur in any presently known documents before the Early Dynastic period. In spite of the presence of terms for "slave," in other words, there is still no unequivocal evidence for the emergence of a fully developed system of class distinctions at least until the onset of the Early Dynastic period.

By late Early Dynastic times there is much fuller and less

ambiguous evidence to suggest the existence of just such a system. It can best be documented, of course, from contemporary written records, but to rely on them alone would overemphasize the contrasts with earlier periods for which they were not available, thus perhaps also overstressing the disjunctive aspects of change during the Early Dynastic period. So let us consider first the archeological evidence.

Architectural exposures sufficiently large to provide a meaningful picture of differentiation in private domestic architecture occur only in the Diyala area east of modern Baghdad. To judge from ancient Eshnunna, the larger houses lay along the main roads through the settlement and often occupied 200 square meters or more of floor area. The greater number of houses, on the other hand, were considerably smaller and seem to have been compressed into the interiors of the "blocks" formed by the main streets and the establishments adjoining them, having access to the arterial roads only by means of twisting, narrow alleys. As a result, many of the smaller houses lack the characteristic enclosed court of Mesopotamia houses in general and do not exceed 50 square meters of total area. There is independent evidence in the associated small finds, in one case consisting of a valuable hoard, that the large houses were occupied by persons of greater wealth as well as superior status. Significantly, the largest dwelling was apparently that of a merchant, for opening on the street from the residence behind was a display room with tiers of bins and receptacles.

The impression of differentiation is confirmed and amplified by a study of tomb furniture. One of the clearest indices to wealth is the presence of copper, as well as more precious metals. In part, the increasing quantities of copper found in Early Dynastic graves may reflect only an enlargement in supplies reaching the lowland cities, but the previously unparalleled concentrations of metal that appear in a few graves nonetheless must indicate a correspondingly increased range of differentiation in wealth. And while copper becomes "*le métal d'échange par excellence"* by the Early Dynastic III period (Lambert 1953:208), on the whole it remained of so high a value that ordinary craftsmen and even minor bureaucrats were limited to at most a few implements of this material for which they were at pains to keep an accounting. The bulk of the peasantry may not have benefited from the increasing supplies at all, for none of the utilitarian copper implements connected with agriculture that have been recovered so far apparently was made earlier than the Akkadian period. In other words, copper implements and vessels (to say nothing of gold or silver) qualitatively increase the implication of wealth for the burial assemblages in which they occur, as opposed to those in which they are lacking.

In the Early Dynastic I period, there already was greater variation in the kind and amount of accompanying grave goods than had occurred previously. At Kish, for example, burial equipment for the ordinary grave still consisted of a few large spouted jars and other pottery vessels, with no weapons or ornaments; but an unspecified, presumably small, number of graves contained copper daggers, lances, axes, sling missiles, stone and copper vessels, copper mirrors and toilet articles, and the like. Although not representing great concentrations of wealth when compared with the royal tombs, the luxury character of many of the burial offerings is evident. There are copper stands or trellis supports, for example, which are found exclusively in association with stone vessels in some of the wealthier burials. At contemporary rates of exchange, the weight of copper wire in the trellises would have been sufficient to purchase a field large enough to provide a modest livelihood, yet each of the stone vessels found in a support could stand unaided.

A somewhat later development roughly corresponds with the late Early Dynastic II and III periods. It is known most spectacularly from the so-called "Royal Cemetery" at Ur, although contemporary finds at Kish and Khafajah confirm the same general pattern and provide some hundreds of additional graves as examples. At Ur, 588 burials have been described that were not connected with "royal tombs." Of them, about one-eighth lacked metal or stone objects of any kind, while an additional 751 graves, although they yielded no offerings suitable for dating, must be roughly coeval with them. Here we see the remains of a peasantry presumably maintaining itself only slightly above the margins of subsistence, physically associated with an urban center but having acquired few of the tangible symbols of its wealth or technological progress.

On the other hand, about twenty seemingly non-"royal" graves contain a substantial wealth of offerings: personal ornaments of gold and silver, large numbers of well-made stone and copper vessels, beads of gold and lapis lazuli, gold bowls, gold- and silver-mounted daggers, quantities of bronze tools and weapons, etc. Below this extreme, but intergrading with it to form a relatively smooth curve of distribution, were considerably more numerous graves that, on the average, contained several copper and bronze tools and utensils (mirrors, strainers, razors, bowls, axes) in addition to pottery, an assortment which Sir Leonard Woolley (1934,2:164) somewhat offhandedly characterizes as "typical middle class." In all, 434 of the graves at Ur have some metal and 167 have objects of gold and silver, a very high proportion of the 588 clearly datable graves and a respectable proportion of the total even if all the undated graves are assumed to be contemporary.

In sum, insofar as grave goods reflect the general distribution of wealth, there is evidence for a decisive increase in social differentiation in the cities during the course of the Early Dynastic period. It did not take the form of a numerous elite that was sharply cut off from an undifferentiated mass of artisans and peasantry. Instead, it appears that the resources of the royal family frequently were only slightly superior to those of a few great private houses and that in the main urban centers the latter, in turn, graded off gradually to various degrees of impoverishment.

It is interesting to contrast this concentration of wealth at Ur with the situation obtaining in the contemporary, nearby site of al-Ubaid. Of 94 recorded burials there, only 18 contained any metal at all, only 4 contained more than a single metal object, only 1 contained objects of precious metal, and no grave contained more than 3 metal objects. Al-Ubaid, it would seem, was a rural dependency of the capital at Ur, with much of its wealth drained off to support urban specialists and administrators.

Whether this was generally the case with the rural population—and, indeed, how much of the population lived in outlying, dependent villages—is a question that cannot be answered, in view of the exclusive concern of Mesopotamian archeology heretofore with the greater aesthetic appeal, and greater promise of finding texts, in the cities. Large numbers of villages do occur in the northern part of the alluvium, but that region, Akkad, differs both culturally and ecologically from the region of Sumer in which most of the classical Sumerian city-states were located. There are textual references to temporary structures near the fields that were occupied by Sumerian agricultural workers during the harvest season, and it is at least possible that many small settlements like al-Ubaid were consolidated into larger, more defensible urban centers either just before or during the Early Dynastic period. On the other hand, several centuries later than the Early Dynastic period, the little Sumerian kingdom of Lagash is reported to have comprised some 25 towns and 40 or more villages and hamlets within a 1,600 square kilometer area. If so, something of the same pattern may have persisted from Protoliterate or earlier times right through and beyond the initial impulses toward urbanization.

The conclusion from the archeological evidence that late

Early Dynastic society was a stratified, class system is confirmed and amplified by the contemporary written records. At least its quantitative characteristics can be best understood by a study of differences in ownership or control of land, but the Shuruppak and Lagash archives also provide information on some of the duties, perquisites, and relative positions of the various strata.

At the bottom of the social hierachy were slaves, individuals who could be bought and sold and who seemingly were owned in small numbers even by some ordinary artisans, agriculturalists, and minor administrators. Their economic role was a much more significant one, however, in connection with great estates and temples, of which the Bau archive furnishes so richly documented an example. In the Bau community of some 1,200 persons, there were from 250 to 300 slaves, of whom the overwhelming proportion were women. One tablet alone lists 205 slave girls and their children who probably were employed in a centralized weaving establishment like one known archeologically at the site of ancient Eshnunna; other women are known to have been engaged in milling, brewing, cooking, and similar interior operations permitting close supervision. Male slaves generally are referred to as igi-nu-du, "the blind ones," and apparently were employed in gardening operations. Although there are no direct references to the blinding of war prisoners to prevent their escape, it is a possibility that at least remains open.

While it has sometimes been maintained that slavery as an institution was of minor, almost insignificant, importance in ancient Mesopotamia, there are two respects in which this view must be contradicted. In the first place, even if the gross proportion of slaves was relatively small, we have just noted that their distribution throughout the economy was highly uneven. In the Bau archive, representing a great estate or temple, perhaps one-sixth of all resources available above the subsistence level were devoted to the production of wool and thread. Moreover, slaves working under semi-industrialized conditions played a preponderant part in this process, and the sale or exchange of this commodity not only played an important part in the local redistributive economy but presumably also served as the basis for long-distance trade in luxuries and vital raw materials like metal. In a sense then, there was a strategic concentration of slaves in precisely those institutions which characterized Mesopotamian urban society as distinguished from preurban society, so to characterize the institution as insignificant, accordingly would misrepresent its importance as a factor in development.

A second argument for the strategic importance of slavery has recently been persuasively elaborated by Moses Finley (1964). His essential point is that the data from the Old World, both Near Eastern and Classical, does not reflect a polarization of society into slaves and free citizens but, instead, a wide spectrum of alternative possibilities. Legal, social, political, and economic criteria of dependence or subservience may overlap and contradict one another, but there was a cumulative movement until Classical times toward more and more sharply defining and isolating a dependent stratum of foreigners at the bottom of the social hierarchy. In fact, it is only with this development that the abstract contrast of "slavery" with "freedom" emerged at all.[2]

The implication of Finley's analysis for our present problem is that it is perhaps inapropos to reserve the term "slavery" for the group I have just discussed, on the implicit assumption that it is sharply contrasted with a much larger "free" population. Instead, there were various social impediments and conditions of servitude, of which slavery was merely the most extreme, and the role of an inferior and in some respects unfree agricultural class was surely far more important than the numbers of nar-

2. A "freed" slave, the term meaning literally that it was "returned to its mother," was first mentioned in Urukagina's time, at the end of the Early Dynastic period (Edzard 1965: 80).

rowly defined "slaves" alone would suggest. Seen in this light, the controversy between Soviet economic historians characterizing early state society as "slave" society and Western specialists insisting on the relatively small numbers of slaves in some respects becomes more a matter of nomenclature than of substance.

The so-called "shub-lugals," of whom there were about eighty in the Bau community organized in groups under overseers or foremen, are an example of a group with a reduced status and degree of freedom. The term has been variously translated as "subjects of the king" or merely as "subjects of a master," but in any case their clientage is apparent from their duties. In various texts they are reported as laboring in gangs by the day on demesne lands of the Bau temple or estate, pulling ships, digging irrigation canals, and serving as a nucleus of the city militia (perhaps specialized slingers or archers) under the direct command of the palace administration. Two muster rolls that have been preserved make it clear that upon the death of a shub-lugal he was succeeded by a near relative, who assumed his same duties under the same overseer. By the time of the Bau archive at about the end of the Early Dynastic period, shub-lugals were among many groups who received a subsistence ration during four months of the year in return for labor service. The shub-lugals also were allotted small plots of prebendal land from holdings of the temple or estate. There are indications that further control over the group was maintained by the periodic reallocation of the plots, even though their size indicates that many of them would have been inadequate for subsistence purposes.

There are other groups that basically resemble the shub-lugals, although differing in their economic position and apparent degree of clientage. The uku-ush, who perhaps served as heavily armed shield- and spear-bearing units in the phalanx formations of the army, also served as overseers for the shub-lugals on labor assignments but were bound by approximately the same conditions of service. More ambiguous are the positions of engars and sag-apins. Engars have been described variously as "clients" and "free peasants," but in any case both titles can at least be assigned somewhat higher positions in the social hierarchy; they conducted or supervised agricultural operations on behalf of the estate or temple, supplied cadres for the militia, and received both rations and allotments of prebendal land. None of these groups could be bought or sold, it must be stressed, although the clientage of a number of shub-lugals in Lagash may have been involuntarily transferred from the city ruler Lugalanda to his successor, Urukagina.

Clearly, there was not a single status of clientage but a series of perhaps overlapping ones based on distinctions that are not yet apparent. And it is admittedly dangerous to generalize from the limited and selective archival sources at present available. particularly in view of their disproportionate emphasis on the larger (especially temple and palace) estates with scribes in their employ and special managerial problems for which permanent accounts were almost a necessity. If Diakonoff's estimate (above, p. 65) is correct, as much as two-thirds of the population in late Early Dynastic times still was not directly dependent on manorial units at all but was organized instead in corporate kin communities. However, it does seem reasonable to conclude that at least on agricultural estates the labor force consisted primarily of this semifree gurush class, whom I. J. Gelb has likened to Greek *metoikoi,* Roman *glebae adscripti,* and English serfs.[3]

Even on lands apparently not falling within the bounds of great temples and estates, there are suggestions that small private plots were not held in alodial tenure but were subject to certain forms of entailment. They could be sold and transferred, as we know from many examples at Shuruppak, but nevertheless they stood in some relationship to a superordinate

3. Gelb 1964. But cf. Gelb 1965: 240–41, where the closeness of the comparison is reconsidered.

institution—probably the administrative establishment of the city ruler. Plows and even seed corn were provided by this central authority, a practice that apparently can be traced back as far as Protoliterate times on the basis of a tablet of that date from Tell Uqair. The notarization of a dub-sar-gan (field scribe), who must have been a representative of this establishment, was an integral part of every purchase contract. Moreover, it may be noted that sales occur in rigid multiples of 2.5 iku (0.88 hectare). One might suspect on this basis that sales were not entirely at the discretion of the individual owners but were subject to a degree of superordinate control that the documents took for granted and therefore do not mention.

Large-scale private acquisitions of land have already been mentioned. Perhaps the earliest example known is the so-called "Blau Monument," long regarded as a forgery prior to the discovery of pictographic Protoliterate writing in secure archeological contexts. The purchase of 250 or more hectares by one Du-si and of at least 114 hectares by Lu-pad, a high official of Umma, are later, better understood examples, while the acquisitions in four districts that are recorded by one Akkadian king on the "Obelisk of Manishtusu" total 2,300 hectares and those by Enhegal of Lagash amounted to about 1,000 hectares. Most if not all such purchases seem to have been made by members of ruling families or high officials, and the documents recording them are appropriately described as *"Sammelurkunden";* that is, they are records not of the simple transfer of integrated large holdings but of the assembling of such holdings out of many separately owned, small parcels.

Thus the implication of an ongoing process of concentration of landownership in the hands of state officials during at least the later Early Dynastic and Akkadian periods cannot be doubted. In the case of the lands Manishtusu purchased, to be sure, they were redistributed to relatives and political supporters rather than being directly worked by their new owner. But that is unlikely to have been the case even with royal acquisitions before the wide conquests of the Akkadian period, and the king's correspondingly increased responsibilities for the defense of distant frontiers. And archives of a considerable number of Akkadian estates, privately owned and yet often employing on rations up to several hundred dependent agricultural workers and their families, make it clear that the trend in general was not toward redistribution but toward the growth of large, directly managed holdings.

Of a still larger order of magnitude than the acquisitions just cited were the estates already in the hands of the ruling officials of the palace and temple. The Bau archive is one of these, and in fact is the main source and prototype of Anton Deimel's reconstruction of an all-embracing *Tempelwirtschaft*. Now, as we have seen, Deimel's conclusion that units similar to the Bau temple virtually monopolized the available agricultural land has been shown to be untenable. Moreover, current studies even cast into some doubt his interpretation of the Bau community as subordinated in any significant way to the service of a particular god or a temple hierarchy.[4] But Deimel's calculations of the total size of the establishment, about 65 square kilometers of arable land under the direction of an administrative official responsible to the wife of the Lagash city ruler, nevertheless seem entirely reasonable. Although much less is known of them, similar records of large landholdings can be traced back into the Protoliterate period; a fragmentary tablet from Jemdet Nasr accounts for 1,828 hectares and may have originally contained a much larger total.

Of course, the management of a manorial estate of this great size could not be fully centralized irrespective of whether it was conducted in religious or in secular terms. As we have seen, some of the estate lands were cultivated directly on its behalf by shub-lugals; on the basis of known proportions for a very small part of its area, the demesne lands might amount to about one-fourth of the total. Another, larger portion consisted of the

4. John Hadley, personal communication.

prebendal lands allotted to members of the Bau community, the harvest from which presumably was devoted very largely to their own subsistence. By far the largest of such allotments was an area of some 348 hectares that also was cultivated on behalf of the city ruler and his wife by the shub-lugals, but, while other high officials also received generous amounts of land, most allotments were very small. Still a third portion consisted of rent lands, which were farmed on a share-crop basis, again largely by members of the Bau community, and which constitute almost half of the lands whose relative proportions can be accounted for.

Even the share-crop lands were centrally supplied with seed, draft animals, equipment, and specialized personnel for plowing. Moreover, accounts of receipts and disbursements suggest that about thirty storehouses were centrally managed— in one of which alone the presence of 9,450 tons of barley is recorded. Hence the Bau administration should not be construed as a political structure superimposed on a pattern of atomistically conducted agricultural operations merely to facilitate the passive collection of taxes or tribute. It was, in fact, an *oikos* in the classic Weberian sense, an authoritarian super-household in which a remarkably differentiated labor force of clients undertook to provide their lords with goods and services. Although little is known in detail of the earlier development of this integrated, consumption-oriented economy, it may be noted that the distribution of rations was already accounted for, presumably in exchange for labor services, as early as late Protoliterate times.

Drawing together the many diverse strands in this discussion of social stratification in early Mesopotamia, I believe we can trace the emergence of a fully developed class society by no later than the end of the Early Dynastic period. Its origins, prior to the appearance of cuneiform documents, can be followed only indirectly, in the gradual emergence of a difference between richly furnished tombs, on the one hand,

and the much more numerous graves of a relatively impover-
ished peasantry, on the other. Subsequently, however, we can
establish the internal gradations within this society more and
more clearly from written sources. The system of stratification
was, of course, closely articulated with systems of political and
military powers and prerogatives, but those relationships must
be reserved for consideration in the following chapter. Here our
major concern is the economic basis of stratification, particularly
as defined in terms of degrees of servitude and access to land.

Standing at the pinnacle of Mesopotamian society were
small numbers of princely families who seem to have been
vigorously extending their control of land by purchase during
the later Early Dynastic and Akkadian periods. There has been
a tendency at times to define the role of such families somewhat
too narrowly in terms of their administrative duties. Leo Oppenheim, for example (while admittedly addressing his remarks in
the main to a somewhat later period), recently has broadly
characterized Mesopotamian society as notably lacking in the
elements of a military aristocracy and even of "any non-economic
status stratification" (1964:74-75). Were this really the case,
the absence of these features would represent an important
contrast with Aztec society in central Mexico. But I think it
can be replied that we simply lack the kinds of sources in
Mesopotamia—at least until long after the Early Dynastic period
—that might be expected to refer in any way to special behavi-
oral characteristics and prerogatives setting off the elite from
the mass of the population. The emphasis on official functions
in existing records is no more than a reflection of the fact that
the overwhelming majority of these records are themselves
narrowly administrative in function. We may deplore the absence of interpretive descriptions by visiting interlopers who,
like the Spaniards, tried to record all they saw. But a proper
comparison of Mesopotamian with Aztec society requires that
we take their absence fully into account.

At any rate, ruling families in Mesopotamia seem to have

headed semi-integrated manorial estates that varied greatly in size. Their labor force, dependent in varying degrees on the distribution of rations, allotments of land, and other forms of clientage, also included a small but significant proportion of persons employed under repressive, closely controlled conditions of outright slavery. Yet, in spite of the proliferation and increasing importance of these class-oriented forms of organization, there still existed kin-based communities both outside and within the manorial establishments, and, while such communities were declining in the relative amount of land under their corporate control, it is likely that they still had very large areas at their disposal.

This was, in short, a complex, changing amalgam of older forms of social organization and new ones. But it is important to remember that the older, kin-based institutions were not merely pushed aside by patron-client relationships, to decay slowly along the neglected margins of the latter. As in the case of the continuing role of kin ties in the administration of army and labor service, clientage, and the crafts, the older forms at least at times were readapted and retained as important structural features. As Julian Steward observes, this is only common and natural; "simple forms, such as those represented by the family or band, do not wholly disappear when a more complex stage of development is reached, nor do they merely survive fossil-like, as the concepts of folkways and mores formerly assumed. They gradually become modified as specialized, dependent parts of new kinds of total configurations" (1955:51).

For several reasons, the prehispanic Mexican system of social stratification can be much more briefly treated than can that of the early Sumerians. It is, in the first place, better known, having been studied and debated since the early days of the discipline by a succession of leading anthropolgists. Second, because of the availability of Spanish descriptions of Aztec society at the height of its power and prosperity, the lengthy processes of inference required to reconstruct an integrated system of Sumerian stratification from unrelated fragments of archeological data, land deeds, and bookkeeping entries can be vastly simplified. And, third, there is simply less information with which to trace the development of the institution through its long incipient stages than in the case of Mesopotamia.

Although we know of burials at Teotihuacán ranging from simple, unceremonious inclusions in construction fill to moderately well-endowed tombs and of a corresponding variation in domestic architecture, the accidents of archeological discovery have provided us with no later burial and architectural sequences from which quantitative evidence might be obtained on the extent of social differentiation in successive periods. Equally important, there are no Mexican parallels for the voluminous Mesopotamian economic records, from which at least certain conclusions relevant to social organization can be drawn as early as the Protoliterate period and which shed increasing light on the many centuries that followed. Taking into account these differences in the documentation for the two areas, we can only describe the Aztec system as the Spaniards encountered it, briefly noting short-term developmental trends toward statification to which the traditional accounts of the growth of the Aztec realm refer. Even on this limited basis, there are striking and fundamental similarities to Mesopotamia that are immediately apparent.

Recent discussions of land tenure by Alfonso Caso (1963) and Paul Kirchoff (1954) provide essentially similar overviews that for the sake of brevity may be followed closely. At the apex of the Aztec social pyramid stood the polygynous royal household, its line of divinely descended Tlatoanis marrying daughters of the leading chieftains of the realm to produce in time a largely endogamous nobility sharply differentiated from the rest of the population in wealth, education, diet, dress, and other prerogatives. While these pillis, or members of the nobility, comprised the upper echelons of the political and military administration, they were lords, as Zurita says (1941:

90-91), " by virtue not of dominion or command, but of lineage."
Large numbers of them—600, according to Cortés (1952:96),
as well as their servants and followers—were constantly in
attendance upon the royal court, where they were maintained
with support from the state treasury.

In addition to an impressive flow of tribute from subjugated
towns, a subject to which we must return subsequently in connection with the emergence of political and military authority,
there were great estates at the king's disposal comparable to
those in early Mesopotamia. Apparently a distinction was
recognized between patrimonial lands, which belonged privately to the king as a result of inheritance or conquest, and
entailed lands set aside for the maintenance of administrative
personnel and other specific purposes. Except that this distinction illustrates nuances of administrative usage that would be
preserved for us in the interpretive reports of a Spanish chron-
icler but not in the deed prepared by a Sumerian clerk, it is
not of great importance for understanding the economic basis
for class stratification and the royal power. Both categories
certainly were very large. Moctezuma I is alleged to have
held some thirty-two towns and twenty-six estates for his
private benefit, and it is reported that the three kings of the
Triple Alliance reserved for their own use at times as much as
one-third of the huge extent of conquered territories. Still other
state lands apparently were given over to temples and schools
and cultivated by tenants or were set aside for the support of
garrisons and war expenditures.

Private lands were also held by the nobility. In some cases
they were apparently subject to various forms of entail, and they
reverted to the crown in the event of the death of an owner
without heirs. However, they were subject to sale, and the
produce from them could be appropriated by their noble owners
without the deduction of a share as royal tribute.

The source of all such private lands, it should be observed,
was the successful conquest of neighboring territories. In the

first recorded instance, after the fall of Azcapotzalco in 1430 before the combined forces of the Triple Alliance, Diego Durán (1867-80: 1, 79-80) tells us that the largest and best fields were first taken by the crown, that two plots of land were then given to each of the nobles who had pressed the war against the wishes of the common people, and that for the latter only one plot was set aside for each calpulli. Paul Radin (1920:147) has argued that this award of lands to the nobility was an innovation, but, even if not, it thenceforward assumed special significance because of the almost continuously success-ful expansionistic thrusts upon which the Aztec subsequently embarked. It served to strengthen the hand of the military orders in their struggle for ascendancy over the traditional calpulli leadership and to provide an economic basis for the formation of a noble class that was distinguished from lower social orders by more than transient charismatic qualities and self-proclaimed superiority of lineage.

In addition to an aristocracy of lineage there was an aris-tocracy of service, made up in the main of commoners who had distinguished themselves in warfare. Although beneficiaries of royal favor during the early, rapid growth of the realm, they were later repressed and excluded as the nobility of lineage continued to grow in number during a period when the frontiers tended to become stabilized. Also of an intermediate status, although rising in wealth and influence rather than declining like the nobility of service, were corporate groups of merchants. Since they were engaged exclusively in long-distance trade, largely on behalf of the ruler and the nobility, they were closely involved in the expansion of the Aztec state. Accordingly, we must postpone a discussion of their role and position until the following chapter.

Below these groups a large part (in most regions the major part) of the population was grouped in calpullis, as we have seen earlier—localized clans or lineages that were highly strati-fied internally, that held corporate title to agricultural lands, and that also served as a basis for the organization of many of the crafts and professions. There seems to have been a minimum of twenty calpullis, and probably there were several times that number, with recognized territories in Tenochtitlán at the time of the Spanish Conquest, and there is some evidence that the calpullis were ranked among themselves from highest to lowest.

As the persistence of vertically oriented (i.e., stratified) kin-based social groupings across the growing horizontal barrier between nobles and commoners implies, this was a society embarked upon fundamental change and hence not easily summarized in terms of unifying organizational principles. Even in its ceremonies, M. Acosta Saignes (1946:196-97) has documented the effects of these essentially contradictory developments, with kin-based modes of organization and those reflecting the class superiority of the nobility alternately coexisting amicably and confronting one another in mock battles.

Some scholars, like Arturo Monzón (1949:29), argue from the vital part that the calpulli undoubtedly continued to play that stratification remained so closely intertwined with kinship that we should not speak of social classes. However, the distinction between a stratified society and a class society seems to be an obscure and not particularly significant one—so long, at least, as there is agreement that the direction of development in Aztec society was toward the latter. Classes and clans need not be polar, mutually exclusive concepts, and it is in the general nature of social change that it arises from the competitive coexistence and ultimate resolution of such seeming contradictions.

Below the "plebeian" population of macehuales organized in calpullis stood the mayeques, who cultivated the private lands of the nobility and who (like the client populations on Mesopotamian agricultural estates) have been likened to serfs on medieval fiefs. Probably for the most part having been earlier settlers on the lands to which they became attached, they could be sold with those lands but not separated from them.

Unlike the "free" population of commoners organized in cal-pullis, who as we have seen owed tribute to the state, the mayeques owed tribute and labor services only to the noble owner of the land they occupied. Their only obligations to the state, suggesting the very limited extent of their participation in it, lay in the wartime performance of military service and in their subjugation to its criminal jurisdiction rather than that of the local lord.

The queston of the size of the mayeque population is obviously an interesting and important one, since it bears on the extent of private landholdings and on the degree to which the calpulli system may have begun to decline in at least its economic importance before the arrival of the Spaniards. Direct, unequivocal data are unfortunately not available. Calculations based on the imposition of tribute on previously exempt classes of the indigenous population after the Conquest do seem to suggest, however, that in parts of central Mexico the mayeques were very numerous and may even have outnumbered the population of the calpullis (Cook and Borah 1963).

Presumably mayeques also tended to be organized into localized, endogamous calpullis, or at least once had been so. Both the periodic breaking up of private lands through pur-chase and the formation of new mayeque groups out of impov-erished families and refugees would have reduced the relative importance of kin ties among them and substituted more flex-ible, open-ended organizational forms. Their way of life as a whole, however, received little attention from the early chron-iclers and is not well known. According to one source, which describes the depression of these groups to the lowest margins of subsistence, tribute payments to the lord were handled as individual and not corporate responsibilities, with those who failed to meet the requirements being sold into slavery. This practice also would have hastened the decay of corporate kin organizations among them.

Slaves constituted a bottom stratum in the society, and, as

in early Mesopotamia, their absolute number was seemingly not large. Recruitment is said to have depended mainly on impressment of criminals, on defaulting debtors, on self-sale during times of famine, and, in some cases, on their requisition as tribute. It differed from the classical Western concept of slavery as an unlimited condition of depersonalization and servitude and constituted instead a social category whose status was only somewhat more impaired than that of the mayeques and similar groups. Slaves are reported to have been engaged, alongside other workers, in the cultivation of private lands. However, on public lands and in the construction of public works, corporately recruited corvées of tributaries and the internal calpulli population provided both a more flexible source of labor and one that was largely self-sustaining from a subsistence point of view; hence it is not surprising that the use of slaves for these purposes is unreported. Similarly, there is no reference to their employment in the crafts.

There were two areas of strategic concentration of slaves in the Aztec economy, recalling their similarly discontinuous distribution in Mesopotamia. In the absence of draft animals in the prehispanic New World, it is not surprising that one of these concentrations was in the transport of commodities, although even in this case slaves failed to supplant "free" carriers in the delivery of the tribute to which subject towns were obligated. Slaves also are repeatedly reported to have been very numerous in the great households of the nobility, although here too they merely supplemented and did not replace the obligated services of tributaries.

There are suggestions that the number of slaves was increasing during the last decades before the Conquest. Both the increasing degree of autocracy and stratification within the core of Aztec society and the increasing flow of tribute, including slaves, from conquered towns make this a probable trend even if we are unable to document it in quantitative terms. But if so, it may be asked whether increasing numbers of slaves merely reinforced existing social relationships or whether instead they began to have qualitative effects on the socio-political structure. Unlike mayeques on nobles' estates, whose surplus product went only for the support of their lords and might not be attached as tribute, slaves in the hands of the commoner population would have served to augment state revenues. Hence the issuance of slaves to commoners would have tended to counterbalance the loss of potential sources of tribute through the award of conquered lands and their attached agricultural populations to the nobility. At the same time, the forging of further links of this kind between the state and the calpullis would enhance the trends toward stratification within the latter and would help keep in check the independent powers of the nobility.

To hazard a larger and more speculative conclusion from a comparison of slavery in early Mesopotamia with that in pre-hispanic central Mexico, one is first struck by many formal and functional similarities: the relatively small number of slaves, their discontinuous distribution throughout the economy, their apparent concentration particularly in the service of the political and economic elites of the society, the absence of abrupt dis-continuities between slaves and numerous other groups of impaired social status. Beyond these similarities, however, are suggestions of an important underlying difference that may be traced also in the origins of the nobility and of their control over land.

We have described the great Mesopotamian estates as semi-integrated, implying that their owners or administrators employed at least a degree of comprehensive management and planning in order for resources to be made available in sufficient amounts and with sufficient regularity to justify the retention of substantial numbers of slaves in economic production rather than merely in service functions. By contrast, the Aztec nobility seems to have been almost exclusively military in origin and predatory in effect. Characteristically, they sacrificed both war captives and slaves on a scale, and with a degree of ritual elaboration, which elsewhere was quite unprecedented. However elaborate their rationale of social superiority may have been (and, parenthetically, our ignorance of a corresponding rationale in Mesopotamia may be only a result of the different character of our available sources), the Aztec nobles seem to have received land exclusively as royal gifts in return for political support or military prowess—that is, for reasons unrelated to their economic functions. Cortés tells us that all the nobility, as well as the royal court, were housed for at least part of the year in the capital (1952:92-93), and, to judge from all available evidence, that city was larger and more heavily populated than any of the city-states of early Mesopotamia. In spite of the ease of communication by boat within the Valley of Mexico, in turn we must assume (particularly in the absence of draft animals) a substantial diversion of labor merely to the task of transporting provisions to the nobility and the court. Meanwhile, the techniques of agriculture remained primitive and unspecialized, undoubtedly differing from one zone to another but at any rate not encouraging the division of the labor on a single crop into specialized operations for separate work teams like those known from the Shuruppak and Lagash archives.

Thus the conditions for the nobility to exercise a role in economic management were largely absent, while their preoccupation with expansionistic warfare along distant frontiers would have precluded their acquisition of the necessary skills. Hence it is no surprise to find that, as Charles Gibson (1964:263-64) reports, the holdings of individuals in central Mexico were often widely separated; the only role open to the nobility in respect to land, after all, was the imposition of onerous tribute schedules. In Mesopotamia, by contrast, we have already noted that *Sammelurkunden,* deeds recording the formation of territorially consolidated estates, were the dominant form of transaction in land.

All of which is, of course, merely another way of asserting

the contrast already alluded to between stratification as a mechanical, politically superimposed process on the African model and stratification as an organic process intimately inter-related with agricultural management. Yet this difference is not large in relation to the accompanying similarities. From the viewpoint of stratification, it is not too much to describe early Mesopotamia and central Mexico as slightly variant patterns of a single, fundamental course of development in which corporate kin groups, originally preponderating in the control of land, were gradually supplemented by the growth of private estates in the hands of urban elites. And, while such corporate kin groups still remained active and viable in many respects at the termination points in our two sequences, it is only fair to conclude that they had by then become encapsulated in a stratified pattern of social organization that was rigidly divided along class lines.

IV

PARISH AND POLITY

THE RESTRUCTURING OF STRATIFIED CLANS ALONG CLASS LINES HAS
a vital but indirect relation to the growth of the state. Older,
vertically oriented, solidary forms of organization were replaced
by more functionally specified, authoritarian, and all-encom-
passing horizontal ones that were better adapted to the administrative requirements of increasingly large and complex
societies. In some respects the older forms may have provided
a model that the newer ones needed only to readapt and sys-
tematize; such was the case in connection with the extension
of the traditional labor and tribute system from within the
calpullis to meet the needs of the emergent Aztec state. But
an analysis of the state, and of the class system on which it
was based, nevertheless are more than complementary approaches to the same unified reality. Their paths of development obviously intertwined and reinforced one another, but
in important respects each followed laws of its own. To intro-
duce a dramatic simile, what we have followed thus far in
discussing the growth of social stratification is the action of
the chorus—its conflicts and resolutions somewhat diffuse and
gradual, broad in impact, but always impersonal. Now we
must deal with the central protagonists.

The first to appear were the priests—or, at any rate, an elite
whose claims to leadership were primarily validated in religious
terms. Shrines and small temples surely long antedate the
beginnings of our chronological chart. In fact, for the New
World at least, Gordon Willey (Braidwood and Willey

120

1962:350) has argued that they may be as old as the establishment of settled village life. But, as the precincts of specialists somehow chosen to lead or represent the community in worship, there is little basis at present for assuming that they antedate the Middle Formative period in Mesoamerica and the Ubaid period in Mesopotamia.

For those remote time periods it must be pointed out again that the data of archeology remains unsupplemented from documentary sources. Religious rituals, it may be argued, are by nature more stylized, repetitive, and capable of association with complex, durable symbolism than are channels of political decision-making and authority. Moreover, it is entirely conceivable that there were other motivations for ritual than religious ones, even in stylized, monumental settings whose formal features identify them as related to known temples of later periods. Clearly, therefore, the dominance of the religious component—or indeed its differentiation at this time from other symbolic forms of social representation and activity—ought not to be merely assumed.

On the other hand, the intensity and omnipresence of predominantly religious forms of expression, and their preponderance over all other surviving traces of social activity not directly concerned with subsistence, are uniformly acknowledged by investigators who have dealt with the era beginning with the Ubaid and Middle Formative periods. Hence the probability of a primarily religious focus to social life at the outset of the Urban Revolution, while often somewhat naïvely exaggerated, appears to be the decidedly most reasonable reconstruction of the available evidence.

Why should this have been so? Part of the answer may lie with the necessity for providing an intelligible moral framework of organization for society as it increased cumulatively in scale and complexity. As Clifford Geertz has recently argued,

A society consisting of a multiplicity of overlapping groups, each directed to a distinct and fairly specific end—a pattern I have elsewhere called "pluralistic collectivism"—would seem to need some ritual expression of the elemental components of its structure in order to maintain a level of conceptual precision sufficient to permit its participants to find their way around in it. The temple system provides both a simplified model of Balinese social structure and a schoolroom in which the kinds of attitudes and values necessary to sustain it are inculcated and celebrated [1964:30].

Although it is hardly possible to elucidate all the specific factors at work in Mesopotamia and Mesoamerica, our earlier discussion of underlying subsistence patterns in the two areas at least suggests what some of the most important of the factors are likely to have been. In the first place, there is substantial evidence from both areas of ecological instability, which has repeatedly been reflected in drouths, famines, floods, and similar disasters. At a magicoreligious level, it is thus no surprise to find that the earliest conceptions of deity to crystallize were those associated with the assurance of fertility and the annual regeneration of crops and livestock.

Thorkild Jacobsen has argued plausibly that in Mesopotamia the name of the goddess Inanna, whose symbol is common on even the earliest Uruk seals, may be derived from her association with the ripening dates. The etymology of Dumuzi, he suggests, is "he who quickens the young ones," and he interprets representations of Protoliterate ritual as already reflecting community celebration of a sacred marriage ceremony between them (1963:474-76). Other authorities, more cautious about projecting the contents of later myths so far into the past, deny the attribution of the ceremony but uniformly acknowledge the prevailing identification of the earliest known deities with the life-giving powers in nature. Eridu, the earliest city to emerge out of the primeval waters in the Sumerian creation epic, was the seat of Enki, god of the sweet waters. The name of the god Ashnan is a word for grain, of Lahar for sheep, and of Sumugan for flocks of wild asses and gazelles.[1]

1. Miguel Civil, personal communications.

The motif of the rosette-shaped flower, apparently symbolizing vegetable life in general, prevails alike on Protoliterate temple façades and as food tendered to divine herds on Protoliterate seals.

This phenomenon corresponds closely with the prevailing religious emphases throughout the long "Classic" period in central Mexico. Perhaps the central conception at Teotihuacán, for example, was the god usually identified by his later Aztec name, Tlaloc. He was variously depicted on murals with attributes of a jaguar, a serpent, a feathered serpent, a butterfly, an owl, and a shell, and René Millon (n.d.) observes that "he was apparently conceived not solely as a god of rain but as a god of life, of living things, a life-giving god." Whatever the precise attributes of this conception, in each instance there is reflected a pervasive and protean preoccupation with fertility, and particularly with the fertility of the major sources of subsistence. Although harder to define, other deities whose associations are at least suggested at Teotihuacán include an earth god, a maize god, an old fire god, and others.

It is interesting to note that in both Mesopotamia and Mexico gods were conceived, or at any rate depicted, in anthropomorphic form, though it is a gross generalization and conceals a considerable underlying divergence. In Mesopotamia the earliest representations of Inanna apparently were in terms of her symbol only, while the human practitioners of her cult were realistically portrayed. Very shortly, however, the gods were also represented as humans, and only a horned crown can be said unequivocally to distinguish a deity. Special areas of concern or competence were assigned to various deities, as we have seen, which in at least one instance—the association of Inanna with the planet Venus—can be established directly rather than from presumably retrospective accounts in later myths. But, in general, all the available evidence forms a consistent picture of a pantheon whose members, from the latter part of the Protoliterate period onward, were endowed with divine powers but who otherwise were characterized by the ordinary human appetites, failings, and emotions. In central Mexico, on the other hand, the incredible wealth of mural art at Teotihuacán suggests that the gods were more remote and awesome in their powers, more closely identified with the demoniacal and animal attributes with whose masks and features they were clothed, and surely less human either in their relations with one another or with man. The beginnings of propitiatory human sacrifice, even if on a relatively modest scale as yet, only serve to underline this difference.

Yet, in spite of this partial contrast, the appearance of generally anthropomorphic forms may not be without significance, for in both instances we confront under similar circumstances, and hence must seek to explain, the emergence of representational art in cultural traditions where it had been almost entirely lacking during the immediately previous eras. Since in both cases the representational portrayal of deities seems to occur somewhat later or at any rate with less clearly anthropomorphic attributes than the portrayal of human figures, perhaps this trend is associated not so much with the elaboration of a great religious tradition as with the ongoing process of social stratification. In short, perhaps it was the emergence of an elite—whether secular or sacred makes little difference—that promoted those aspects of individuality for which portraiture became necessary as an enduring symbol and monument.

Powerless as man might be before the major disasters, the emphasis on the building of temples and the formation of priesthoods undoubtedly also reflects a more "rational," economic aspect. In the absence of widely extended political controls, offerings brought to a sanctuary in aggregate would have constituted a larger reserve than otherwise could be attained, a reserve transcending the environmental limitations of its parent community and reflecting the advantages of complementarity to be derived from establishing a network of permanently related communities in adjacent ecological zones.

For reasons already suggested, Mesopotamia met this challenge in one way and central Mexico in another. In the former, the temple developed not only as a sanctuary but also as a redistributive center and a focus of managerial activity. In the latter, attention was turned outward, overcoming great distances, as well as the absence of long navigable waterways and draft animals, with an astonishing hyperdevelopment of interregional exchange or "trade." In neither case is it necessary to argue that the socioeconomic importance of the function fully "explains" the enormous growth of temples as architectural complexes and as consumers of a major share of the available surplus in the form of subsistence goods and luxury products. Their socioeconomic contribution at one time might be shown (but only in the complex, reified calculations of an external observer) to have been very nearly equivalent to their consumption, or again it may not. All that I would insist on is that their genesis is likely to have involved elements of a direct economic contribution by the temples to the well-being of their communities, as well as a perhaps more clearly perceived and deeply felt religious one.

Let us consider the character of temple activities and organization somewhat more fully for our two respective areas, both as it existed soon after the outset of the Urban Revolution and as it began to change toward the end of the era of Theocratic Polities, the Urban Revolution's first phase.

In Mesopotamian temples we can trace a broad trend toward both an increase in size and an increasing differentiation in function. There are some embarrassing loose ends suggesting that this process may not be an entirely regular and irreversible one (e.g., an enigmatic exposure of what may have been an imposing public building at Tell Uqair as early as the Ubaid period), but on the whole the evidence from the half-dozen or so sites where temples are known—and above all from Uruk—forms a consistent picture. Well before the end of the Protoliterate period both the resources and the administrative skills for building on a truly monumental scale were clearly in hand; according to one authority, the labor force required for the sub-structure of the Anu Ziggurat alone at Uruk was 7,500 man-years. Perhaps even more important, there was a transition from the reduplication of separate, traditionally planned structures that were seemingly oriented exclusively toward ceremonies to functionally specialized, interdependent complexes that included attached living quarters for their attendant personnel and tended to be set apart as a separate precinct by an enclosure wall. The hypothesis of a progressive detachment of the per-sonnel of the temple from direct involvement in the life of the community herein finds considerable support.

After making due allowance for the far greater emphasis that Protoliterate temples have received than all other contemporary structures of a secular character, it remains clear that they were the dominating architectural features of the urban centers growing up around them. And, in at least partial return for the agricultural surpluses they absorbed in the gods' service, it is also clear that they were the crucial centers for innovation in such specialized administrative skills as writing and the keeping of accounts. The first application of writing was, in fact, to the keeping of economic records within the temple. Soon afterward it was extended to the preparation of lexical lists, including lists of gods. Writing remained technically primitive and hence limited in application until the latter part of the Early Dynastic period, but as early as late Protoliterate times knowledge of its application for purposes of keeping accounts would have strengthened the managerial functions of temples. On the part of the specialized groups to whom knowledge of writing was confined, it would also have encouraged a sense of detachment from and superiority to the day-to-day concerns of secular life.

Temples also seem to have been the chief innovative centers for at least the crafts that depended on expensive raw materials from distant sources. Among them were metallurgy, stone sculp-ture, and perhaps the more specialized subdivisions of carpentry concerned with boats and with wheeled transport. While an economic contribution from the sponsorship of these innovations cannot be denied, it also must not be overemphasized. It appears from documentary sources, for example, that extensive practical use of carts began more than a millennium after their introduction for cultic and military purposes.

On the whole, the picture is one of an extremely precocious development on a relatively limited scale. Glyptic art, for example, seemingly leaped into being almost overnight. From the first, it maintained uniformly high standards of workmanship that were never surpassed and displayed what Henri Frankfort (1939:23) describes as a "creative power . . . such that we meet among its astonishingly varied products anticipations of every school of glyptic art which subsequently flourished in Mesopotamia." Typically, its splendid early products seem to have been designed exclusively for administrative and ritual purposes within the temple establishment; it was only toward the end of the Protoliterate period that the functionally interrelated complex of writing, seal-making, and the use of seal impressions was extended to secular economic uses elsewhere. Similarly in the case of metallurgy, the finest early work reflects full control of all major alloys and techniques save a knowledge of bronze and devotes itself to the limited but highly exacting production of ritual furniture. Tablets found in temple contexts from the latter part of the Protoliterate period already differentiate, it is interesting to note, between the position of the smith and that of the master-craftsman who was his supervisor.

A study of the organization of the Protoliterate temple encounters serious handicaps. The graves of specialists associated with the temple are unknown, or at least unrecognized, eliminating a valuable potential source of insight into their status in relation to the community as a whole. While representations of offering rituals and other cult activities are fairly numerous, the fact that many of the participants were nude deprives us of information that otherwise might have been obtained from differences in their dress. And even the Protoliterate documents, so helpful with respect to specialization within the crafts, provide at best a series of administrative titles whose authority and responsibilities are not specified.

At least in Uruk and probably elsewhere as well, the figure at the head of the temple community in Protoliterate times, in both its secular and its religious aspects, seems to have been the en, or lord. Such a figure is shown taking a central part in cult and military activities, distinctively dressed and of heroic size, but his superordinate position in relation to a priestly hierarchy is not apparent. Until the functions associated with the title changed in Akkadian and later times, Dietz Edzard (1965:74-75) observes that it denoted not a priestly office but a broadly politicoreligious one. Even in relation to the temple economy, Jacobsen defines its concerns (admittedly not on the basis of contemporary references) only as "successful economic management: charismatic power to make things thrive and to produce abundance" (Jacobsen and Kramer 1953:181).

Our difficulties are not lessened with respect to other officials who occupied a place within the temple administration. One of those most commonly met on the early Uruk tablets, for example, is the sanga, sometimes translated as "priest" but by other authorities only as "accountant." Before the end of the Protoliterate period several ranks of sanga can be distinguished at Jemdet Nasr, but in the context of a puzzling, poorly understood architectural complex, which in some respects is more suggestive of a "palace" than a temple. It is perhaps more instructive to note that a ration list from the Eanna temple precinct at Uruk accounts for a day's beer and bread allotment for almost fifty individuals, presumably in its current employ or at any rate in its parish following, while other fragments record the consumption of barley and fish. Here, in a clearly religious setting of Protoliterate date, the centrally administered redis-

tributive patterns typified by, and best understood in, the Bau
archive several centuries later thus were already in existence.
Having developed in such a setting, of course, there was nothing to prevent many of the same patterns from being adopted
in time for the administrative purposes of the palace or of
private estates.

So far, we have considered early Mesopotamian religious
patterns without reference to their geographical distribution.
The fact that all the major gods in the later pantheon were regarded as having their principal sanctuaries in particular cities
clearly points back to a time when they were closely identified
with particular places or districts and were correspondingly
limted in their assumed radii of efficacy and importance. Yet
this time must have ended early, since the later myths are consistent in conceptualizing the members of the pantheon as a
hierarchically organized interacting family. The head of that
family, Enlil, resided at Nippur, a city important subsequently
as a symbol of political control and a center of religious learn-
ing but apparently never a capital. Presumably, the explanation
lies not in the forcible extension of local cults by politicomilitary means, of which there is no trace in the available evidence,
but in the establishment of interconnections between the administrative staffs of different temples as they sought to sys-
tematize a common Great Tradition and to solve common
administrative problems.

In this sense, it is interesting to note that even the earliest
known forms of writing were not localized; an example has
been found at Kish, in the northern part of the alluvial plain,
as well as in Uruk, near its southern extremity. Toward the end
of the Protoliterate period, word lists, the characteristic means
of instruction of Mesopotamian scribes, were set down in identical order at Jemdet Nasr (also in the north) and at Uruk. At
least at the level of the specialized elite, it thus appears that
a conscious unity of outlook, a sense of qualitative distinctive-

ness in relation to other, non-civilized areas, had been forged under theocratic auspices well before the advent of the first serious attempts at political unification.

Less can be said with respect to the overall organization of temples, and of the theocratic elite that presumably was identified with them, in central Mexico during the "Classic" period than in Protoliterate Mesopotamia. Teotihuacán stands out as an urban center of a qualitatively different order of size than any we know or reasonably can anticipate in Mesopotamia, and, in spite of a generic similarity to the latter in its theocratic overtones, this difference in size is associated with other important differences as well. Teotihuacán exhibits, for example, an imposed unity of plan on an enormous scale (nearly 30 sq. km. at its maximum) that is entirely foreign to Mesopotamia. Its undeviating grid of equidistant streets intersecting at right angles (at least from the Xolalpan period onward), its emphasis on regularly planned compounds facing inward upon enclosed courts, its mastery of dramatic effect in the arrangement of long lines of temples flanking the main approaches as one moved toward the central shrines, and, finally, the magnitude of effort represented by the Pyramid of the Sun and the Pyramid of the Moon and by many other structures, all are entirely without counterpart in Mesopotamia.

We are on more familiar ground when we turn from comparisons based mainly on scale to others based on function. For many, and perhaps most, of the enclosed compounds it seems reasonable to infer a primarily residential purpose, and the preoccupation with religious themes in their mural decoration may signify only the still undifferentiated character of religious, social, and political idioms. Like the Eanna precinct in Uruk, the largest of the great enclosures at Teotihuacán contained both ceremonial and residential structures (the so-called "Ciudadela," but possibly there are similar enclosures around each of the two major pyramids) and may have served as residences for the principal ruling families. But what of the many smaller compounds, which are still impressively large and lavishly decorated? Are they residences for an inordinately larger priesthood than Mesopotamian cities ever knew? Or perhaps the palaces of an aristocracy drawn from an immensely wider hinterland than at least the Protoliterate and Early Dynastic cities ever had? Or do we exaggerate the status of their occupants, many of whom conceivably could have been internally stratified, densely settled corporate kin groups instead of a noble stratum with quarters for many servants? The answers to these and similar questions depend on studies still under way at Teotihuacán.

The picture also remains obscure with regard to the role of Teotihuacán temples in the crafts. René Millon (n.d.) has recently outlined an attractive but still tentative argument in favor of viewing a great compound adjoining the Pyramid of the Moon as one of several centers of specialized workmanship in obsidian. More generally, it has often been noted that the "Classic" period as a whole is characterized by marked differences in style and pattern of circulation between ritual objects and utensils intended only for mundane use, with the former receiving a far higher degree of specialized care and circulating much more widely. But these impressions remain to be systematized and fully understood. Perhaps, we can argue, the demand of Teotihuacán temples for obsidian, jade, quetzal feathers, and similar luxury products (not to speak of lime plaster and cotton, which were also imperative needs of the lay population) was directly analogous to the demand of Protoliterate temples for copper, precious metals, lapis lazuli, stone, and cedar wood. But there are also suggestions of differences, which recall the less economically engaged, more strictly acquisitive character of the later Aztec elites (see above, p. 117), Teotihuacán ritual objects exhibit a high quality of style and craftsmanship, but they do not advance in technique or experiment with the possibilities of their material. Nor is there any evidence of managerial activities directed toward the sustenance and improvement of the crafts. Characteristically, systems of numeral notation, and possibly other kinds of glyphs as well, were known but were applied only in an apparently rather minor way for ritual rather than for administrative purposes.

As in Protoliterate Mesopotamia, the conclusion seems relatively certain that political and religious systems of authority were largely undifferentiated at Teotihuacán. Throughout the occupation of the site the major building activity was on structures of a preponderantly ceremonial character, and both the lavish production of ritual goods and the general preoccupation with religious themes tend to confirm the impression that political leadership was predominantly theocratic in orientation. Nevertheless, the sheer size of Teotihuacán, and of the still unknown but presumably large supporting territory under its influence or control, strongly suggests that the prestige of the city as a focus of voluntary pilgrimage and offerings must have been increasingly supplemented by superordinate controls of a more strongly politicomilitary nature.

Armed figures from Teotihuacán, presumably accompanying a trading party rather than bent on conquest, were already represented on an Early Classic Maya stela from the important contemporary center of Tikal in the Petén rain forest of Guatemala. There is also evidence from the highland Guatemalan site of Kaminaljuyú of the importation of such large quantities of Teotihuacán pottery that the possibility of seizure of political control by warriors from central Mexico must be voiced, in spite of the very great intervening distances across difficult terrain. Somewhat later, weapons began to make their appearance in Teotihuacán murals. Military orders of warriors, including those of the Eagle and Jaguar as well as others, now also find their way into representations—however long they may have already been present as a social force before receiving artistic and theological recognition. Finally, there is evidence that the partial abandonment of Teotihuacán before 750 A.D.

involved elements of destruction and looting, suggesting military action, pronounced internal unrest, or both.

Thus a further axis of comparison between Mesoamerican sites like Teotihuacán and their homotaxial equivalents in Mesopotamia involves internal trends leading to systematic change rather than static characterization. In both cases the key development was an apparently gradual rise in the power and influence of militaristic groups, closely accompanied by the transformation of a solidary social organization composed of ascriptive segments into a hierarchical, increasingly autocratic one. The rate of this change, to be sure, was not the same; the designation of the period within which Teotihuacán falls as "Classic" properly implies a substantial, independent aesthetic achievement as well as considerable duration, while its Protoliterate counterpart in Mesopotamia emphasizes instead a more transitory stage in a developmental sequence. But the essentials of the trend, culminating in the rise to power of politically fragmented Toltec groups, on the one hand, and in the increasingly sanguinary internecine warfare of Early Dynastic Sumerian city-states, on the other hand, were the same in each case.

This assertion of parallelisms admittedly is not without difficulties. Detailed comparisons are obscured by an apparent break in the continuity of occupation at many sites in the Valley of Mexico after the fall of Teotihuacán, with different patterns of regional authority perhaps centering for a period on Cholula and Xochicalco before the foundation of Tula. Moreover, Tula itself reportedly was made up of two or more ethnically distinguished population strata, with at least the political and religious reins of authority in the hands not of previously urban groups but of tribalized peoples moving inward from near the frontiers of cultivation. This kind of ethnic amalgam occurs later in the relative Mesopotamian sequence also, but it was not a feature of the first polities in which militaristic elements became dominant.

In spite of these difficulties, the comparisons between Tula and its Early Dynastic Mesopotamian counterparts are very close. We can deal with them, of course, only in the aggregate, as they represent cumulative changes, while recognizing that such cumulative trends almost certainly proceeded at different rates in different centers and everywhere consisted of a complex interplay of retarding and accelerating forces. In fact, the decisive characteristic of the Toltec period is its contradictory aspect, entirely consistent with its transitional position between the relatively stable, theocratically oriented society of the early Classic period and the vigorous, dedicated expansionism of Aztec times. Perhaps this aspect is clearest, as Armillas (1951: 29) has pointed out, in the spread of the Quetzalcoatl cult to centers as distant as Chichén Itzá in Yucatán and to the highland Quiché in Guatemala. The *object* of the cult was an archaic, agricultural, at least formerly peaceful, deity. But its new social content, unlike its form, was the rationale of a warrior aristocracy who, if they failed to construct a durable, politically integrated realm, nevertheless were successful as independently organized military parties in imposing themselves over widely scattered Mesoamerican peoples.

The actual extent of the Toltec domain, not to speak of the effectiveness and continuity of whatever political control actually was exercised by the capital, is left unclear by the vague, semilegendary references to which the historian of the Toltec period is limited. The beginning of the *Historia Tolteca-Chichimeca* speaks of twenty towns or ethnic groups constituting the hands and feet of "Great Tollan," and the known position of some of these towns or groups in later times suggests that the realm may have extended to the Gulf Coast in the modern states of Veracruz and Tabasco. On the other hand, there is always a possibility of a foreshortened time perspective in such references, so that the identification of some localities as Toltec may have stemmed from their temporary occupation prior to the foundation of Tula or from later migrations of epigonal groups after its fall. According to the highly questionable statement of Ixtlilxochitl, the Toltec realm extended "from one sea to the other" toward the end of that dynasty's hegemony, with its final dissolution having been caused in part by an uprising of three principalities along the Gulf Coast.

As in Teotihuacán, temples seem to have dominated the center of Tula, and the religious motivations of its ruling groups may well have continued as strong as they were earlier. But the religious emphasis shifted, as Walter Krickeberg observes, no longer deriving "its essential traits from the divine priest-king, nor from the gods of water and vegetation . . . but from celestial warrior-gods" (1964:229-30). Moreover, the symbols of the Eagle and Jaguar warrior societies, associated with the sustaining of these gods through the securing of prisoners for sacrifice, now became a dominant motif in temple reliefs. There are also representations of the warriors themselves, armed no longer only with spear-throwers but with bows and arrows, the latter probably newly acquired from nomadic peoples to the north.

The confused and somewhat contradictory accounts of the dynastic succession at Tula permit a variety of conflicting interpretations, of which the alternatives propounded by W. Jiménez-Moreno (1958) and Paul Kirchoff (1955) are perhaps the most important. The latter seems to be a more closely argued, and hence generally persuasive, position. Perhaps it is rendered more plausible still by its attribution of the ascendancy of the followers of the god Tezcatlipoca only to the end of the occupation of Tula, for the excavator of Tula has noted the absence of a single representation of that god on structures excavated there (Acosta 1956:107).

Following Kirchoff's reconstruction, then, we see the authority at Tula divided between a sacerdotal ruler who was closely identified with the god Quetzalcoatl and a temporal ruler, with hereditary succession applying only to the latter office. The precise details of the ensuing conflict between these figures are not relevant for us here, save that they seem to reflect a schism within the society between followers of the traditional deity and those of Tezcatlipoca and that the latter, who succeeded eventually in expelling Quetzalcoatl, were committed to a god directly bound up with the practice of war and sacrifice. But the general situation depicted by these admittedly semilegendary sources—most of which is consistent also with the Jiménez version—clearly involves the shift away from sacerdotal or divided leadership toward the ascendancy of militaristically inclined leaders responsive to deities more appropriate to their outlook. It may be noted, moreover, that at least part of the confusion of the sources seems to arise from a continuing tendency for both sacerdotal and temporal rulers to be closely identified with the gods they represented or even to be regarded as deities themselves.

Here is a situation that, obscure though it may be in many of its details, profitably can be compared with Early Dynastic Mesopotamia. Perhaps it might be described loosely as the onset of tendencies toward secularization in a polity previously dominated by theocratic influences, but that description overlooks the probability that the partisans of the new militaristic cults were as deeply impelled by religious convictions as were the followers of Quetzalcoatl. The solution of this impasse lies not in an impossible post hoc measure of religious intensity but in an assessment of the social constituencies each deified protagonist represented—in one case, a theocratic elite with a wide, passive following; in the other, corporate groups of leading warriors seeking to consolidate their position as an aristocracy through control of political and religious authority and through conquest. As S. N. Eisenstadt might describe it, what was truly distinctive of the latter was not a lesser degree of religious intensity but the pursuit of autonomous political goals and the quest for power not embedded in the structure of traditional ascriptive groups.

The sequence of development in Mesopotamia of a politically based institution of kingship is one that also remains obscure in many details but which nonetheless exhibits a basic and striking similarity to central Mexico. Throughout most of the Early Dynastic period the extent and character of the conquests of individual Sumerian city-states remain as elusive as they do in the Toltec legends. Tales like "Enmerkar and the Lord of Aratta," for example, hint at hostile relations between a lord of Uruk and his counterpart in a distant mountainous principality, recalling the shadowy achievements and allegorical milieu of Toltec conquerors. But, while retrospective, semilegendary accounts comparable to those dealing with Tula are available in the form of myths and epics, with rare exceptions they are preserved only in late, highly redacted versions. Hence it is desirable, instead, to trace Mesopotamian developments mainly from the evidence of contemporary titulary.

En, or "lord," already dealt with, appears in the earliest Protoliterate writing and, at least in Uruk, continues until the Early Dynastic II period to denote both political leadership and a religious responsibility for control over the generative forces in nature and for management of the temple estate as a god's demesne. Subsequent to that time, only the priestly aspects of the office were retained. The term for king was lugal, literally "great man" and thus essentially secular in etymology, although the occupant of the office also assumed cult responsibilities and administrative control over the temple. The word lugal occurs once on a text at the end of the Protoliterate period, but whether in its more generic meaning of "master" (as Diakonoff suggests) or as a specific indication of kingship (as Falkenstein suggests) is uncertain. At any rate, it gradually became the general expression for paramount political leadership during the Early Dynastic period and was retained as the single royal title thenceforward. A third title, ensi, alternates with lugal during the Early Dynastic period, connoting essentially the same responsibilities but perhaps acknowledging some external suzerainty. It is not necessarily linked etymologically with the earlier title, en, and may also reflect distinctive local traditions in some city-states. The term continues as an assertion of at least local independence until the time of Gudea, just prior to the Third Dynasty of Ur, whose inscriptions suggest that it may have implied even then some of the qualities as a charismatic provider of abundance that previously had been associated with the en. Later it declined in importance and came to mean an appointive city-governor.

There are obvious parallels between this succession of titles and the apparent division of powers between sacerdotal and secular rulers at Tula, as well as in the ultimate hegemony of the latter in both cases. And there are further parallels with respect to tendencies toward deification and toward the establishment of a principle of hereditary succession. During the Early Dynastic period no kings seem to have been regarded as gods during their own lifetimes, to be sure, but Lugalbanda and Gilgamesh were posthumously elevated to this role. Moreover, there is no reason to assume that the frequent assertion by rulers of divine parentage—for example, "the beloved son of Ninhursag"—was an entirely meaningless epithet. A personal claim of divinity seems to have been made first by Naram-Sin during the Dynasty of Agade and continued to be sporadically reasserted by kings of the Third Dynasty of Ur. Hereditary succession, a right also assigned to the temporal ruler at Tula, is recorded and sanctified by the Sumerian Kinglist. Moreover, an epic tale about Etana, the founder of the First Dynasty of Kish, credits him with having fulfilled his destiny to find the "plant of birth" and bring the institution of kingship to mankind. Such varying indications as these surely suggest a common tendency to buttress the position of an essentially secular authority with divine sanctions and powers.

So far, I have dealt only with the transformation of essentially theocratic authority into political rule. But the fragmentary evidence has been convincingly interpreted by Thorkild Jacobsen (1957) to suggest that other kinds of political organs also had been present earlier and underwent similar processes of displacement as royal powers increased and became institutionalized. Signs for "elder" and "assembly" already occur on Protoliterate texts, and sporadic references suggest that the poorly understood institution they represent continued to play an increasingly circumscribed political role until many centuries later. Unfortunately, we know of its activities almost entirely through literary sources—some are myths, sufficiently remote from their tellers to be projected entirely into the world of the gods, while others are epic tales that surround a nucleus of historical fact with semilegendary episodes concerning kings of the Early Dynastic II and III periods. Such sources obviously must be treated warily, but it is significant that the assembly in the myths occupies a place of predominant importance. Sometimes said to be composed of all the gods and sometimes apparently differentiated as to age and authority, its actions on occasion included the rendering, and even the execution, of judgments. More characteristically, it met in response to a situation of crisis and temporarily delegated extraordinary powers as a war leader to one of its number.

It seems entirely plausible to infer the existence of assemblies functioning along these lines in the Protoliterate period, at the same time as temple communities were functioning under their ens but prior to the establishment of fully constituted dynastic rulers. If the assembly was composed of the heads of the major corporate descent groups in a particular center, it would constitute a council of elders almost exactly like the council of calpullecs, which was the dominant political authority among the Aztecs at the founding of Tenochtitlán in the fourteenth century. In areas closely adjacent to the Aztec capital such councils continued to exercise similar powers until the time of the Spanish Conquest.

By contrast, the situation portrayed in the Early Dynastic epics is one in which the presumed descendants of earlier war

leaders had succeeded in varying degrees in assuming a position of permanently elevated status and authority. The beginnings, at least, of the formation of an independent economic
base, in the form of the acquisition of lands by the palace,
have already been referred to. Furthermore, all the available
evidence—the circumvallation of most or all of the major towns,
the increasing emphasis on chariots and weapons in tombs
and graves, the importance of representations of activities associated with warfare on funerary and other monuments, and,
of course, direct textual references—clearly indicates the increasingly serious, chronic character of the military activities
to which the appointment of a war leader had been an initial
response. At least in part because of the greater defensive
strength of large, densely nucleated settlements, and perhaps
partly also because of the greater political control that could
be exercised over them under such circumstances, it also appears that this was a time of the transformation "des agglo-
mérations centrales en véritables 'cités'" (Falkenstein 1954:
810).

Such a process is exemplified by Enmerkar, described in
the Sumerian Kinglist as "the man who built Uruk," while his
father is listed only as the "king of Eanna" (Jacobsen 1939:86).
Like Kulab, a neighboring town whose name is listed in earlier
texts from Ur apparently in place of Uruk, Eanna subsequently disappeared as a political entity, although literary
echoes of it persisted. Presumably both, perhaps together with
unnamed smaller dependencies, had been induced or compelled
by Enmerkar to come together within a newly constituted
urban framework. Surely in such a situation the traditional
powers of the formerly separate assemblies would tend to
weaken collectively, while those of the king would grow more
secure.

Yet forty years later his successor in the kingship of Uruk
was still constrained to share with an assembly his decision-
making powers concerned with warfare. Gilgamesh, although

now holding his office by divine appointment rather than by an edict of the assembly, was forced to plead for the approval of the Elders for a war with Kish. Having been turned down in this effort, an early literary account relates that he succeeded in imposing his will only after convoking an assembly of the young men and winning their support. The king's role, in other words, depended upon a combination of charisma and maneuver before which the legislative organ gradually retreated into passivity and then disappeared as a significant political force.

Alonso de Zurita provides a report of a strikingly similar transitional process among the Aztecs:

The killing of a merchant or a royal messenger was regarded as a justification for war. The ruler would call together all of the elders and the warriors to consider this course of action, informing them that it was desired to make war on a particular province and what the reason for it was. If it was for one of the indicated reasons, all said that this was justified and that the cause was sufficient. If it was for another, lesser reason, they indicated two or three times that war should not be declared, and on some occasions the rulers acceded to their wishes. But if the ruler persisted and they were called together repeatedly, they said that they would follow his wishes, that they had now informed him of their opinions and would disclaim further responsibility [1941:107].

As the pomp and authority of the Aztec Court at the time it was encountered by the Spaniards suggests, the form of this exchange conceals the emerging content of fully constituted royal authority. Several steps can be discerned in the process of its growth, perhaps beginning with Itzcoatl's initial victory over the Tepanecs of Azcapotzalco and the following distribution of conquered lands to provide an independent economic base both for the crown and for the nobility. Immediately thereafter, the Codex Ramirez reports a revision of the customs pertaining to the succession, with the elevation of the nearest brothers and relatives of the reigning king to a new princely rank from which alone his successor could be chosen (by a senate which narrowed to exclude even most of the nobility). The decision taken at the same time to burn the picture histories recording the past practices and humble origins of the Aztec elite, because "it is not suitable that everyone should know the pictures" (Leon Portilla 1959:11) can best be understood as an aspect of this same process.

With the spreading conquests of Aztec armies and the consequent further accretion of strength to the king and the nobility at the expense of the traditional calpullec council, increasing social barriers in movement, dress, and behavior were erected not only between the nobility and the commoners but between the king and the nobility. Durán tells of elaborate regulations to this effect promulgated by Moctezuma I (A.D. 1440–69), and the trend culminated under Moctezuma II (1502–20) with the widespread substitution of members of the nobility of lineage for officials whose rank was based on service alone. Many of the latter, including the heads of the Tenochtitlán calpullis, reportedly were put to death in a purge that formally completed the transition, as Paul Radin puts it, "from an elected chief to what seems, to all intents and purposes, a king" (1920: 150).

Given the strikingly parallel overall pattern of the emergence of kingship in these two instances, in spite of the hemisphere and 4,000 years in time that separate them, it is useful to compare the characteristics of the emergent dynastic institutions in more detail. Let us consider first the scale and elaboration of court life.

Palaces belonging to the Early Dynastic II and III periods in Mesopotamia have been partially excavated at Eridu and Kish, each apparently covering substantially more than 100 meters in each direction of massively walled, highly compartmented private apartments for the ruling family and possibly the families of other high administrators or personal servants. Accompanying these monumental, functionally specialized residential structures were other buildings, for the most part not yet identified archeologically. An account from late Early Dynastic Lagash, for example, notes that "the houses of the ensi (and) the fields of ensi, the houses of the (palace) harem, the houses of the (palace) nursery (and) the fields of the (palace) nursery crowded each other side by side" (Kramer 1963:318). Thus the "palace" in the broader sense constituted an economic and administrative as well as residential establishment of considerable size and complexity.

In the Early Dynastic I texts from Ur, a substantial number of specialized palace entertainers and servants can already be identified, including gatekeepers, cooks, stewards, cup-bearers, servants, messengers, male and female slaves, and, since a harem official is mentioned, presumably concubines as well. At Shuruppak, never a large or important political center, the Early Dynastic III archive lists additional positions for musicians, chamberlains, and butlers and numbered several hundred people. On personnel lists kept by the Shuruppak palace, perhaps as records of corvée service, we also learn that there were considerable numbers of craftsmen in at least its periodic employ. Separately grouped under their respective foremen were masons, potters, reed-weavers, clothworkers, leatherworkers, carpenters, smiths, stonecutters, millers, brewers, and perhaps others. The contemporary palace staff at Susa, even without counting slaves, included 471 men and 482 women. With the political unification of the country under the Akkadians, there was a further qualitative increase in palace staffs. We are told of Sargon, the founder of the dynasty, that 5,400 men ate bread before him daily.

In terms of size and magnificence, the Mexican palaces were perhaps even grander. That of Nezaualcoyotl at Texcoco is said to have covered eighty hectares, although much of this great compound was given over to pleasure gardens, administrative offices, armories, and even a private zoo. The palace of Moctezuma II in Tenochtitlán was much smaller, probably as a result of urban congestion in that island capital, but its usable area was increased by a second story, which housed the royal apartments, and 3,000 persons were said to be in continuous attendance upon the king. Also within this establishment were administrative and judicial offices, granaries, prisons, artisans' workshops, quarters for the harem, and, again, a zoo, whose denizens are said to have consumed five hundred turkeys a day. "I will say no more than that there is nothing like it in Spain," wrote Cortés to his emperor. As Jacques Soustelle observes, "these are very strong words from a Spanish hidalgo addressing himself to Charles V" (1962:25).

What differentiates these two instances is a characteristic feature of the economy that has already been touched upon. In Mesopotamia, the ration lists make clear that we are dealing with a permanent staff of palace retainers, presumably supported by its own corps of agricultural clients (e.g., the shublugals), by offerings from temples (the mashdaria texts referred to earlier), estates, and perhaps corporate kin groups and even individuals whose lands lay within the general suzerainty of the palace, and occasionally by booty. By contrast, the Mexican palaces depended in the main on labor service recruited on a rotation basis. Nezaualcoyotl, for example, "had divided the country surrounding his capital into eight districts, each of which was obliged to perform these duties for a given period each year, under the supervision of a calpixqui" (p. 84).

On the other hand, the decision by Moctezuma to limit his personal service to members of the nobility suggests at least the beginnings of an erosion of this old calpulli-based system. Moreover, suggestions of a large relative increase in the class of "unfree" mayeques, with individual responsibilities to their lords for tribute and service (see above, p. 115) point in the same direction. Finally, the mounting demands of the royal court for luxuries led to the provisioning of quarters and subsistence for craftsmen within the palace itself as the conquests of the Triple Alliance continued; in some instances craftsmen were called from all parts of the realm to take up what must be assumed to have been regular services there. Different in detail as these two systems may have been, there is thus reason to believe that they were becoming more and more closely aligned in their major institutional patterns until the Spanish Conquest terminated the development of one of them.

Burial practices constitute another tangible aspect of royal wealth and authority and provide a further interesting parallelism. The "royal tombs" of Ur are sufficiently well known not to need extensive description. Human sacrifice was a conspicuous feature of most of them, with up to seventy or eighty members of the royal retinue accompanying the chief occupant of the tomb. Men-at-arms, ladies of the harem, musicians, chariot-drivers and grooms with their war vehicles drawn by oxen, servants crouched in attitudes of personal attendance—all were present, together with large stocks of costly, beautifully worked objects, which today number among the principal treasures of three of the world's great museums.

As a result of the accidents of discovery, or the effectiveness of post-Conquest looting, no such tombs have yet been found enclosing the remains of Aztec kings. But what there were once, and what may yet be in store for future archeologists, is suggested by a report of Moctezuma I's funeral:

Upon the death of this king he was accorded the appropriate obsequies for rulers of his station, and all the kings and lords of the region attended them with offerings and presents. According to their use and custom they killed many slaves and retainers in the belief that they might serve him in the after life, and they buried him with a great part of his treasures [Durán 1867-80:1,253-54].

Behind such displays as this, and ultimately more meaningful than the suggestions of royal wealth they supply, surely there were basic understandings about the nature of kingship itself that were closely similar, although their details now may be irretrievably lost.

The special responsibility of the royal court for military

affairs—or, perhaps better, the articulate leadership provided by the king and his immediate entourage for the social forces committed to military expansion as a policy—is strikingly evident in both Mesopotamia and central Mexico. In the former, a wide variety of supporting data might be cited. Archeologically, it includes representations of the heroic figure of the king at the head of his troops, as well as the emphasis on weaponry (including costly ceremonial weapons) in the "royal tombs." In historical inscriptions we find the king emphasizing his personal rivalry with rulers of neighboring city-states and personifying his whole force in boasting of sanguinary victories that left the bones of his enemies to the mercies of vultures and hyenas. His special concern with the organization of the army is perhaps less metaphorically shown by the fact that many units of the Bau militia are directly stated to have been mustered under his command, while the responsibility for army personnel assignments seems to have rested with his administrative assistant, the nubanda. Further, of course, the shub-lugals and similar units who seem to have composed the semiprofessional core of the army were personally bound to him in a patron-client relationship. Gilgamesh, perhaps epitomizing the martial attitudes ideally associated with kingship, seems at one point to call derisively for those who are timid or who have domestic responsibilities to return to their homes, while he will venture forth with no more than fifty single adventurers at his side. Rejecting conciliation, he characteristically calls for defiance in the face of Agga's armies sailing down on Uruk in their longboats:

> "Let us not submit to the house of Kish,
> let us smite it with weapons."[2]

2. Pritchard 1950: 45. For an up-to-date critical overview by a number of specialists of what has been called the "Babylonian national epic" see Garelli 1960. This discussion implies a rather discouraging estimate of the potentialities of the literary genre as a whole for any but the most cautious and sophisticated attempts at historical reconstruction.

Identical attitudes are repeatedly expressed in the Aztec chronicles. The frequent insistence of the king on a declaration of war, even over the reluctance of his council because of formally inadequate pretexts, has already been referred to in the testimony of Zurita. Although sacrificial practices may have had a very ancient origin, the enormous extension and elaboration of sacrificial cults in the later days of Aztec conquests seems to have followed closely upon royal command. Such was the case, for example, with the hecatombs of war prisoners—reputedly 20,000 or more—sacrificed by Ahuizotl over a four-day period in 1487 at the consecration of the new Great Temple in his capital. A particularly illuminating expression of militaristic attitudes was provided by Tlacaelel, later the highly influential founder of a line of Aztec "prime ministers" but then a young general prior to his accession to office, at the critical moment of popular indecision within Tenochtitlán leading to the successful uprising against Azcapotzalco and the opening of the way to empire. In the face of moderating council not only from the commoners but from some of the nobility as well, Tlacaelel came forward to exhort the crowd in terms reminiscent of Gilgamesh:

"What is this, Mexicans? What has happened to you? Have you been deprived of all reason? Wait, stop, and let us come to some better understanding about this matter. Who would be such a coward as to have us go and surrender ourselves to the people of Azcapotzalco?" [Radin 1920:94].

It must be stressed again, however, that the close relationship of kings with military activities and with relatively autonomous, essentially political, centers of power in the society continued to be conceived in religious terms in many vital ways, rather than falling easily under the rubric of secularization. With the initiative passing to the political sector, religious institutions and conceptions provide a further illustration of

Steward's dictum about earlier integrative forms not merely fossilizing or disappearing but, instead, tending to become specialized, dependent parts of new kinds of total configurations (see above, p. 110).

Many, perhaps most, of the ceremonies and beliefs of an earlier era surely were retained, but they were cast into a different context and assumed a different significance. Tlaloc, for example, the seemingly omnipresent god of rain and vegetation who dominated Teotihuacán, at best shared the leadership of the Aztec pantheon. Perhaps it is also significant that now he was thought to be located on the peaks of distant mountains and that his role was increasingly confined to that of a patron deity only for the peasantry. Huitzilopochtli, so recently risen that he does not appear among the gods of the calendar, increasingly had come to dominate the pantheon and to provide the principal focus for the sacrificial cult.

In Mesopotamia, Akkadian influences resulted in the addition of several new deities and in certain syncretistic trends, but the principal deities remained the same. Instead, it was the attitudes attributed to them that seem to have shifted, although, admittedly, the evidence for this change has to be derived from later sources, so the time of its onset is uncertain. Enlil, the "farmer," "the lord of the plow," was increasingly identified in epithets instead of as "the lord of all lands" or "he who breaks the enemy land as a single reed," and most other members of the pantheon as well increasingly tended to be viewed not as agriculturally oriented, functionally specified, local figures but in the aspect of celestial warriors. In the process of being transformed into the Semitic goddess Ishtar, even Inanna did not escape this change [Falkenstein and von Soden 1953:32-33].

In both areas, again, the principal temple of a town became identified as the key redoubt of its political autonomy and military resistance. In the literal transcriptions of hieroglyphs prepared for the Spaniards, the representation of a destroyed or burning temple is taken to be equivalent to the conquest of the community, and in numerous attestations from the chronicles the burning of a temple signified the end of all resistance and the victory of the Aztec god. Similarly, the looting and burning of Mesopotamian temples was at least an important concomitant of military victory. An inscription of Urukagina of Lagash, for example, complains that the men of nearby Umma under Lugalzagesi, culminating a long rivalry, had destroyed the statues of his principality's temples and stripped them of silver and lapis lazuli.

If destroyed temples commonly were the symbol of defeat, they also were among the principal beneficiaries of victory. Offerings of sacrificial victims to Aztec deities have already been mentioned. In a Mesopotamian literary tale of the earlier rivalry between Uruk and the Aratta, the submission of the latter is symbolized by the bringing of stone and the building of a shrine in Uruk by the people of Aratta. Records of ex voto offerings of slaves to temples by a victorious king, as well as the explicitly stated right of the god to a share of the booty, are first attested only in the Ur III period on the basis of present evidence but may well have occurred much earlier.

Lest it be thought that the emphasis on the acquisition of precious substances for the enhancement of the cult was the major strategic objective of warfare, it may be noted that Entemena of Lagash also boasted of having exacted some 10,800 metric tons of grain from Umma as an indemnification for unsuccessful rebellion. While this claim may be somewhat inflated, the same ruler's subsequent admission that the men of Umma had seized a storehouse containing 270 tons of grain surely is not. Elsewhere we read of the imposition of a tribute in grain on Enakalli of Umma after his defeat by Eannatum and of the unsuccessful efforts of the former's son and successor to escape from this burden and to reclaim territory that had been lost. In fact, the whole long history of rivalry between Lagash and Umma, extending over more than 150 years, seems to have been based on opposing claims to fields along the border between the two city-states. In addition, there are references, unfortunately only in literary tales whose meanings remain ambiguous, to the possible imposition of corvée duties and even military service on the populations of vanquished towns. Whatever part the defense or gratification of the deity may have played as a conscious motivation for warfare, it is clear that his human protagonists had their own interests in mind as well.

Behind the essentially identical general orientation of religious change, in the two cases, there were also differences that help to illuminate the degree of overall comparison between them. Perhaps as a consequence of the distances between major Mesoamerican centers and the difficulties of communication with exclusively human transport, the Aztec world view was an apocalyptic one that recognized no universal order or stability. In each act of conquest Huitzilopochtli faced another city's god in single encounter, and if the result was foreordained it was at least unknowable to his human protagonists. In Mesopotamia, by contrast, we have seen that the divine hierarchy had already begun to be codified in Protoliterate times and had been endlessly recopied by temple scribes even before the major city-states had appeared on the scene as political rivals. The cosmology, then, was self-enclosing and stable rather than open-ended and in doubt, and the problem of shifting political fortunes had to be reconciled with the collective decision of the society of the accepted gods rather than projected into an essentially unknowable realm of remote and terrible forces. Urukagina, lamenting the fall of Lagash, met the attendant problem of divine injustice in one fashion:

. . . the men of Umma, after Lagash had been destroyed, committed sin against Ningirsu. The hand which was laid upon him he shall cut off. Offense there was none in Urukagina, king of Girsu, but as for Lugalzagesi, governor of Umma, may his goddess Nisaba make him carry his sin upon his neck [Gadd 1962:52].

But for kings in the hour of victory, particularly as those victories spread to encompass all the world as it was comprehended in the Sumero-Akkadian pantheon, the refusal to criticize the acts of the gods and the pious separation between the powers of the divine assembly and their own powers became more difficult. So we find Gilgamesh, in an act of hubris to which there is no parallel in pre-Classical literature, tearing the haunch from the Bull of Heaven and throwing it in the face of his city's goddess with the ringing taunt:

"Could I but get thee, like unto him
I would do unto thee" [Pritchard 1950:85].

Or again, there is a later tale that describes the anger of Naram-Sin when, in the full flood of that Akkadian king's conquests, the gods refused him oracles:

"Has a lion ever performed extispicy, has a wolf ever asked [advice] from a female dream-interpreter? Like a robber I shall proceed according to my own will" [Oppenheim 1964:226–27].

Yet the contrast with Mexico should not be overdrawn. These were the significant but furthest limits of human pride and aspiration, and with their ebb the unattainable, inviolable status of the Mesopotamian family of gods was restored. The epic, after all, tells of Gilgamesh's failure in his quest. And Naram-Sin, having likened his attitude only to that of an animal or outlaw, also soon repented.

In relation to human society, on the other hand, conceptualizations of dynastic power underwent a cumulative and irreversible shift as that power increased. Perhaps the development of the state can best be described as fully consummated when it no longer represented solely the partisan interests of militaristic social strata but began at least to claim a position "above" contending parties. Urukagina of Lagash, for example, phrased his responsibilities to adjudicate the conflicting claims of his constituency for his indulgence and protection in terms of a covenant with the god of his city:

That he deliver not up the orphan and the widow to the powerful man, this covenant Urukagina made with Ningirsu [Jacobsen 1963:480].

This formulation obviously reflects the emergence of at least partially autonomous, impersonal standards of public service, as well as the first steps toward a conception of abstract, impartial justice to which the entire body of citizenry was equally subservient.

Similarly, Zurita observes of the tecuhtli, appointed by the king from the ranks of the nobility as the highest dignitaries of the Aztec state, that "they were responsible for caring for and defending the people in their charge, of defending and protecting them. Thus these lords were appointed to serve the general welfare as well as that of the individual to whom the office was assigned" (1941:86). Zurita also describes the high standards of rectitude and incorruptibility that were expected of Aztec judges, citing a celebrated case in which a Texcocan judge was ordered hanged by the king for having falsified a case in favor of a noble over a commoner (p. 103).

As the foregoing account has hinted at several points, the emergence of the political and economic organs of the state cannot be understood exclusively as a series of internal processes within even the largest urban communities. Both the perils and the rewards of militarism lay beyond the immediately adjoining, more or less permanently attached and dependent, territories. The increasing concentration of political authority in dynastic institutions at the expense of older communal and religious bodies obviously took place in a setting in which both the perils and the rewards of militaristic contention were fully and deeply understood. Successful conquest brought political prestige in its wake, not uniformly enriching the community but, instead, increasing the stratification within it and permitting the consolidation of an independent power base by forces whose initial role had merely been that of leading elements in a common enterprise. In these and many other ways, the consolidation of the institutional structures of the newly developed urban polities must be seen as an internal adjustment to a steadily widening and sharpening context of intercommunity, and even interregional, hostilities.

Hence, having dealt with internal political developments, we must turn to their complementary external manifestations. Unprecedented patterns of extended territorial control were to be found in Mesopotamia as a product of the Akkadian conquests and in the Aztec realm on the eve of its rapid destruction by the Spaniards. The term "empire" is not an entirely suitable one for these patterns in either area; it implies a degree and durability of economic consolidation, as well as of administrative control, for which there is no convincing evidence. Many features we tend to associate with empires apparently were missing or at best very poorly developed, such as royal encouragement of a free peasantry with loyalties directed toward its authority; a mobile, achievement-oriented bureaucracy; policies directed toward the breaking-up of ascriptive landholding units; and the establishment of professional military units whose fortunes were directly linked with those of the state itself. Yet the fact of great territorial extension, and of the taking at least of some preliminary steps toward empire formation, is undeniable. A consideration of the nature and extent of these steps in the two areas will provide a broader basis for the comparison between them.

The evidence on the Akkadian conquests, and particularly on the organization of their realm, is very limited and often ambiguous. Agade, the capital Sargon established, never has been located, preventing a clear understanding from its archives of the respects in which its administrative framework differed from that of the Early Dynastic city-states. Only a relatively modest corpus of contemporary royal inscriptions is known, supplemented by chronicles whose recorded versions are generally of much later authorship, and by omen texts. And although the basic authenticity of the omen texts has been vigorously defended, they are of doubtful meaning and limited utility for historical reconstruction. Even the archeological record can provide little assistance, limited as it is to a few palaces and private houses in towns of lesser importance and to a much smaller and less informative group of graves than are known for the Early Dynastic period. Accordingly, while we are told that "the political organization of the Akkad Dynasty amounted to something of a real revolution in Mesopotamian history" (Finkelstein 1963:464), the precise extent and character of this revolution still elude us.

What does emerge from the available data are a congeries of indications of changing sociopolitical patterns. There was, first, a clear extension of the bounds of territorial control to encompass not only the alluvial plain of lower Mesopotamia but the adjacent regions of Elam, the Zagros piedmont, and Upper Mesopotamia. During the later Early Dynastic period the basis of political strength had consisted merely of individual city-states, held together in fragile alliances only during brief periods of charismatic leadership; now a pattern was imposed that maintained control of a much larger region in one dynastic line for four generations. It was presumably on the basis of firmly established (or repeatedly re-established) domination of the Sumerian cities in the heartland of the realm that the chain of conquests could now be extended outward. As early as Sargon's time it was claimed to have extended "up to the cedar forest and the silver mountains," the Amanus and Taurus ranges, although this expedition perhaps was more a reconnaissance in force than an attempt at permanent incorporation of the huge intervening territory. More doubtful, although not entirely to be excluded, are late, somewhat allegorical claims that there was a still further foray into the central Anatolian plateau to champion the grievances of merchants against the ruler of Purushkhanda.

Also ascribed to Akkadian control, at least in later tradition, were Dilmun (usually identified with Bahrein Island and perhaps the adjoining Arabian shoreline), Magan, in the region of the Gulf of Oman, and Meluhha, variously identified but surely farther still. Separated as they were from the mainland of Akkadian control by a hazardous voyage down the Persian Gulf and possibly beyond, it is difficult to believe that at least Meluhha was subjected to more than minor armed raids. But a literary reference to ships from those regions which moored at the quays of Agade is supported not only by the arrival in Mesopotamia at this time of seals of Indus Valley origin but also by the ample documentation of this overseas commerce—in which Dilmun may well have served as a specialized port of trade—in business records of the Third Dynasty of Ur not long afterward.

Direct references to merchants are rare in the Akkadian inscriptions; such sources as we have naturally tend to view the growth of the realm as an acquisition of power and territory exclusively on the initiative of its central authority. The references which do occur suggest that long-distance trading and tributary patterns were similarly inspired, were directed toward the same geographical regions, and may have been subject to a degree of common administration. At least for the more adequately documented late Early Dynastic period, it can be demonstrated that much of the intercity trade and procurement was either subject to royal demand or under direct royal control. The official status of the dam-gar, or merchant-agents in whose hands it was placed, is suggested by their inclusion on lists of those receiving rations and allotments of land. Moreover, as W. F. Leemans (1950:41) observes, they were organized under a single superior gal-dam-gar official who occupied a high place in the order of precedence of other gal-officials and who seemingly enjoyed an especially close relationship to the ruling family. However, the presence of as many as 32 dam-gar even in a small town like Shuruppak seems difficult to explain solely in terms of royal and religious requirements. And other texts record payments to a merchant by a number of persons on the eve of his departure, suggesting that private trading accounts were beginning to be handled by the dam-gar as an adjunct to their official position.[3] In spite of an absence of confirmation for it in the available Akkadian sources, a further development of this trend during the Akkadian period seems highly likely. In short, while traders were gradually becoming more differentiated and autonomous as a group, patterns of trade probably were still closely interdigitated with exactions of booty and tribute within the spreading realm of Akkadian control.

Sargon's pattern of conquests was essentially repeated by his two sons, Rimush and Manishtusu, who followed him consecutively, and by his grandson, Naram-Sin. Collectively, their inscriptions confirm the impression of a central emphasis on the extension of trade and the acquisition of tribute. Repeatedly we read of conquests whose objectives are suggested by their geographical descriptions: the cedar forest, the silver mountains, the tin (or lead) country, the silver mine. Repeatedly victories were commemorated by temple offerings of some of the captured booty in copper, gold, stone, and timber, with suggestions of direct state support of merchants and commerce. A lament on the downfall of Agade, recalling the halcyon days of the city, quite appropriately speaks of the ships at its quays, of the flow of widely varied goods and offerings in through its gate, and of how this wealth rose like water in the palace magazines (Güterbock 1934:31). Recalling Sargon's victories over a number of Persian Gulf principalities, a motive is supplied by one of his inscriptions, which claims: "Henceforth the ships of Meluhha, Magan and Dilmun freely can come to anchor in the Agade harbor" (Bottéro 1965:107).

More is implied than the sporadic extortion of tribute and imposed trade from distant regions by punitive raids. Far out at Tell Brak, in northern Syria, a great palace built by Naram-

3. Igor Diakonoff, personal communication.

Sin is known, one half of which must have served as the seat
of a local governor and garrison, while the other provided a
secure collecting depot for the transshipment of commercial
or tributary goods. Moreover, Nineveh and Ashur, the major
towns in what later became Assyria, were sufficiently under
the hegemony of the Akkadians for the latter to have founded
temples there; Rimush is even credited with having founded
a "city" in the region north of Nineveh. Accordingly, while
political authority in the further reaches of the realm may
have tended to be thinly and perhaps unevenly distributed,
it cannot be assumed to have been asserted only at infrequent
intervals as an aspect of the capture of booty or the forced
collection of tribute.

A somewhat different picture emerges when we consider
the Akkadian relationship to the traditional Sumerian city-
states in the heartland of their realm. The capital of Agade
apparently was founded in the northern part of the plain, a
region traditionally characterized more by villages than cities,
and many of its settlers must have been seminomadic elements
whose military strength and cohesiveness was in direct proportion to their tribal, non-urban origins. If a conscious
struggle between Sumerians and Akkadians along ethnic lines
apparently can be ruled out by many indications of an absence
of any recognized boundary between these groups in speech,
dress, religion, and political affiliation, nevertheless Akkadian
domination was based on hitherto neglected groups, centered
in a hitherto marginal district, and successfully employed
techniques of domination hitherto unknown.

We learn from their royal inscriptions, for example, of
the systematic destruction of the walls of Sumerian cities that
resisted Akkadian onslaught, an innovation that surely increased the difficulties of reconstituting rebellious coalitions.
This step may presuppose the effective reduction by the Akkadians of local raiding and banditry, against which city walls
also were a defense, although the sources make reference to

pacification only at the level of general rebellion. One of the omens in which Sargon is mentioned speaks of his having settled the sons of his palace for five leagues on every side, suggesting an attempt on a limited scale to create a new kind of landed royal following among certain favored groups of peasantry to defend the approaches to the capital (Gadd 1963:10). An unprecedented emphasis on the taking of prisoners possibly hints at steps to unify the country through the destruction of enclaves of local resistance. This same objective may have been a consideration in the acquisition of royal estates like those notarized on the Obelisk of Manishtusu, for local Sumerian supporters of the dynasty were among its beneficiaries, while others must have been substantially dispossessed. At least some of the major towns, including Susa and Lagash, were additionally subject to the imposition of Akkadian garrisons, and the higher officials of the realm seem to have been exclusively Akkadians. Finally, the occurrence of Urukagina's name as a resident of Agade on the Obelisk of Manishtusu perhaps implies the practice of forcing members of local elites in the other city-states to reside as hostages in the capital.

With all these innovations, it remains to be noted that real continuity of control was never achieved. Sargon seems to have faced a serious, general revolt of the subject cities during the latter part of his reign, and each of his successors in turn—his two sons, Rimush and Manishtusu, apparently having been murdered in palace conspiracies—could resume campaigning along the distant frontiers only after a protracted struggle with the cities immediately at hand. After the time of Naram-Sin, or perhaps even during the final years of his reign, a precipitate retreat from claimed frontiers virtually encompassing the known world began. Sharkalisharri no longer could take the title of "King of the Four Quarters" but instead assumed only the epithet of "King of Agade." After his death, apparently also in the palace conspiracy, the further decline of the dynasty is evident in an obscure interregnum during which there were four contending claimants for the throne. This was, in short, a state whose rulers undertook extensive conquests, created the military means to achieve them, benefited heavily for a time from the resultant flow of tribute and commerce, and made significant administrative advances in the direction of maintaining their authority over a widely extended territory. But their efforts fell decisively short of full imperial control, as the gradual decline and demise of Akkadian suzerainty in the face of relatively limited and uncoordinated incursions of Gutian mountaineers indicates.

In one particularly essential respect the extension of Aztec conquests proceeded along similar lines to those followed by the Akkadians almost four thousand years earlier. The Aztec realm also exhibited a loosely knit quality seemingly in contradiction with the immense armies it fielded against the Spaniards and with the impressive flow of booty its capitals received. Yet, as the inability of the Aztecs to marshall support from among their allies and vassals during the final siege of Tenochtitlán shows, the strength in certain culturally prescribed, largely militaristic, terms concealed but could not overcome the underlying weakness of territorial bonds and the fragility of the political structure as soon as it passed beyond the bounds of the individual town.

While Tenochtitlán had moved into the ascendant political role by 1519, the realm had been originally constituted as a Triple Alliance at the time of the successful uprising against the Tepanecs of Azcapotzalco ninety years previously and, at least in formal terms, remained so until the end. Tribute was supposed to be equally divided between Tenochtitlán and Texcoco, with half as large a share going to Tlacopán; by the time of the Conquest much of it was being redistributed to the other towns only through Tenochtitlán, suggesting that the practice had been changed. As an island citadel formerly without agricultural lands at all, clearly the strategic objectives of

Tenochtitlán differed from those of the Texcocan heirs of the old Alcolhuan domain, with greater need to secure a flow of tribute in subsistence products and with a more urgent demand on the part of the newly emergent nobility for the conquest of lands, their assignment as personal property, and the reduction of their agricultural population to the status of clientage. Not surprisingly, Texcoco was less dominated by the growth of a military aristocracy and continued to concede a role to commoners and merchants in governing councils. But the increasing de facto control of the alliance by Tenochtitlán succeeded in submerging these differences without an open break. Regrettably, the available evidence seems to leave in obscurity the overall flow of goods and services within the Valley of Mexico, including the relationship between the ultimate regional distribution of products received in tribute, on the one hand, and, on the other, the private exchange of craft for subsistence products. Whatever this relationship may have been, the Alliance continued, perhaps increasingly fragile or even empty of content in functional terms but formally intact, until the unprecedented crisis of the Spanish invasion.

In operation, the conquests of the Alliance beyond the limits of its original holdings apparently failed to apply systematically even the limited techniques of control that were developed by the Akkadians. While the supremacy of Huitzilopochtli had to be acknowledged by conquered towns and while a cessation in the flow of tribute from them brought an immediate threat of stern military reprisals accompanied by even heavier demands for tribute in the future, local elites and institutions generally were left entirely intact. There are references in the chronicles to the establishment of garrisons, but except for those along the relatively fixed, vigorously disputed frontier with the Tarascan kingdom to the west, garrisons in general seem to have been posted as additional security for the long-distance trade-and-tribute routes rather than as instruments of political control over conquered populations. Ex-

cept in the longest-subjugated districts forming the strategic
core of the empire, the appointment of loyal Aztec officials
as local governors, displacing native rulers into lesser administrative positions or entirely removing them, was an exceptional proceeding rather than the prevailing one. There are
apparently no references to such techniques of continuous coercive interference as the taking of hostages from among members of potentially hostile local nobilities.

Yet, in spite of this relative thinness in the density of
political controls over at least the outlying conquered territories and in spite of the inordinately heavy Aztec demands
for goods and services as tribute, they were more successful
than the Akkadians in assuring continuity of control. It was
not necessary, for example, for each new king to conquer the
rebellious cities constituting the heartland of his realm upon
his accession—perhaps reflecting, to a degree, the effectiveness
of the demand for thousands of sacrificial victims as a device
for domination through terror, although Akkadian claims to
have slaughtered or enslaved considerable numbers of rebellious enemies apparently failed to have the same effect. A more
crucial difference probably lay in the essential absence of
factions within the Mexican elite, as reflected in the natural
death and orderly succession of Aztec kings in contrast to the
regicides in the Akkadian line. Unfortunately, the stereotyped
Akkadian victory inscriptions and the ambiguous omens and
later chronicles fail to provide an indication of the basis for
these schisms. Finally, the rapidly developing state initiatives
in the construction of irrigation works in the Valley of Mexico
during the final pre-Conquest decades tended to furnish a
material basis for continuing political supremacy—at least of
that key geographic region as a whole, if not of a particular
city or group within it.

It must be remembered, however, that the Aztec regime
was cut short at the height of its powers, while the internal
weaknesses of the Akkadians are magnified for us by the at-

trition they suffered after the reign of Naram-Sin. On closer study, one finds suggestions that similar stresses were developing within the fabric of Aztec territorial control as well. Aztec demands, at least in the onerous and precisely codified form found in the *Matricula de Tributos* as it was applied at the time of the arrival of the Spaniards, clearly had begun to provoke serious unrest among subject peoples—unrest of which the Spaniards were quick to take advantage. In fact, as Bernal Díaz (1960:1, 148) relates, the luxurious attire, rapacious demands, and autocratic behavior of the Aztec calpixques, or tribute-collectors, in Cempoala were among the first impressions the Spaniards received of their future antagonists upon their arrival on the mainland. Moreover, the relatively rapid population increase of the Aztec nobility as a result of the extensive practice of polygyny seems certain, if it had continued for another generation or two, to have produced still more excessive demands for tribute, a centrifugal movement of the nobility into newly established administrative posts with entailed lands away from the capital, and the appearance of internal cleavages comparable to those among the Akkadians.

The limits of Aztec territorial control can be plotted with substantially greater precision than those in Mesopotamia, in the main because the limits defined tributary relationships that the Spaniards themselves were keenly interested in retaining. As Robert H. Barlow's (1949) studies have shown in detail, they disclose a strikingly asymmetrical process of expansion, with the major thrusts carrying far to the south and east, while in other directions the frontiers remained relatively stable. In some cases the explanation is easy; the Tarascans, for example, bloodily repulsed attacks in the direction of Michoacán, while the absence of settlements in the dry zone to the north rendered futile any major expansion there. But elsewhere hostile states like Tlaxcala were allowed to survive as enclaves close to the heart of the realm, ostensibly to provide an opportunity for military training and for the acquisition of war prisoners as sacrificial victims, easily accessible to the captal. Even Tlatelolco, Tenochtitlán's sister-city, was not forcibly brought into the realm until 1473. It is also noteworthy that the conquest of the province of Xoconusco in 1486 led, not to any apparent subsequent emphasis on occupying the intervening territories between this detached and distant area and the main body of the realm, but only to the securing with garrisons of the trade route leading to it.

The essentially chivalric and ceremonial overtones to warfare during the earlier stages of Aztec expansion seem to have been substantially replaced with more implacable and destructive hostilities after the time of Moctezuma I. However, there was little corresponding development of a strategic concern, at least in a sense comprehensible today, in the consolidation and extension of territory. Whether a departure from Akkadian thought and practice is thus represented is by no means certain. We simply lack the kinds of sources in Mesopotamia that might be expected to reflect discontinuities in territorial control, while the Spanish sources tend, if anything, to overemphasize them in Mexico.

Perhaps even to a greater degree than in Mesopotamia (or is this again only a reflection of differences in our sources?), Mexican militarism was closely bound up with interlocking long-distance trade and tribute patterns. Anne Chapman (1957:122) has argued that in most recorded instances trade was followed by tribute, that is, after the incorporation of a province into the realm the activities there of the powerful group of pochteca, or traders, came to an end. If really the case, it would imply that later requisitions of tribute were heavy enough—even on the peripheries of Aztec military control—to eliminate all potential surpluses that otherwise might have served as trading objectives. It is worth noting, however, that there are no indications of the beginnings of a reduction in the numbers or prosperity of the pochteca as their activities were replaced by tributary relationships. Moreover, specialized lowland commodities like cacao sometimes were demanded as tribute from subjugated communities even in the central highlands, suggesting that there were unrecorded processes of tangential and centrifugal circulation of goods alongside the centralized, centripetal ones with which most of the Spanish sources deal. Hence it is perhaps more likely that long-distance trading and tributary patterns considerably overlapped one another. But of their close and complementary relationship to the goals of military expansion there can be no doubt at all.

Recalling the less substantial tales of interventions by Akkadian kings on behalf of merchants venturing beyond the frontiers of territorial control, it is interesting to note repeated instances in which the mistreatment of merchants, or even simply the refusal to trade, served as the pretext for Aztec attack. Indeed, "the documents make it clear that a refusal to trade or the breaking-off of commercial relations was considered to be tantamount to a declaration of war" (Soustelle 1962:204). Moreover, some of the pochteca entered hostile regions in disguise, serving as spies in anticipation of subsequent Aztec invasion, while in other cases members of this group undertook the pacification of a region even without military assistance. Not surprisingly, we learn from Sahagún's account that a monarch like Ahuitzotl (1486–1502) addressed them as "my beloved uncles" and "made them like his sons" (1950–: Book 9, 5, 19). If in fact they had not yet acquired many important perquisites of nobility by the time of the Spanish Conquest, there is little reason to doubt that in some respects their rapid rise had begun to reduce the distinction to a purely formal one.

For the same reason that territorial patterns of control were of such keen interest to the Spaniards, they also meticulously preserved Moctezuma's tribute lists. From them we learn, in a far more complete and accurate fashion than is possible for Mesopotamia in any period, of the organization of tribute as an economic system, including the demand for the delivery in the capital of specified types and quantities of goods at regulated intervals. The quantities are very impressive; the bulk foodstuffs alone are calculated to have amounted to perhaps 52,800 tons, or enough for more than 360,000 people at the estimated mean annual consumption. Moreover, the enormous flow of cacao beans, cloth mantles, and other goods serving as media of exchange placed additional instruments of economic superiority not only in the hands of the palace but in those of the nobility and even of the capital population at large.

Centrally redistributed through the palace, this wealth not only strengthened the autocratic features of the political structure but also heightened class stratification and urban-rural differences. Quantitative estimates of the patterns of distribution unfortunately depend on hotly debated assumptions about the size of the urban population and on the degree to which Tenochtitlán retained more than its stipulated share of tribute. However, it is suggestive of the power of the palace under these circumstances that, according to perhaps as reasonable an estimate as any, some 25 per cent of the cacao, 50 per cent of the salt, and 15–20 per cent of the maize was directly consumed within that institution. Thus it is only reasonable to conclude, as Friedrich Katz puts it, that "the whole economy of the city rested on tribute" (1956:96, 106). Whether this characterization also applies to Agade still remains entirely uncertain.

If we contrast the Akkadian and Aztec imperial systems at a more general level, the essential character of both as trade-and-tribute systems, with only limited tendencies toward centralized administration, stands out immediately. The differences that have been noted seem to imply a somewhat greater degree of direct control on the part of the Akkadians, which in reality may be no more than an artifact of differently oriented and inadequate sources. Given the considerably more integrated character of the great palace, temple and private estates controlling much more of the land in Mesopotamia than the equivalent holdings of the nobility in Mexico, it would not be surprising if there were a somewhat greater involvement of the Mesopotamian state in an economic managerial role. The techniques and even the records were at hand, after all; they only needed to be centrally applied. Yet as the Aztec disbursement of royal stores and construction of aqueducts and irrigation systems in response to famine shows, the Mexican state upon occasion also did undertake productive economic investment, rather than merely consume a portion of the tribute its predatory activities had brought and redistribute the rest to its followers. If there is a difference at all, in other words, it is surely not one of kind but only one of degree.

A more clearly demonstrable difference concerns both military and economic patterns. In the Mexican instance, the major nuclei of settlement were separated by wide expanses of difficult terrain, and communications were further impeded by the absence of navigable waterways and domesticated animals for transport. Military activity accordingly assumed a predominantly raiding character, with the limited logistical supports generally precluding positional warfare and prolonged sieges. Fortification systems, on the whole, seem to have been poorly developed, although, as Angel Palerm (1956) has observed, the major centers may have been able to rely on defenses in depth involving multiple-purpose structures not easily recognizable in their ruins today. In the absence of bronze weaponry, no apparent basis for technological superiority in warfare existed, so the successful Aztec pursuit of an expansionistic policy had to depend exclusively on higher levels of skill, organization, morale, and numbers than their neighbors could muster.

The pattern the rulers of Agade inherited from the Early Dynastic city-states was a more sophisticated one. Cities were customarily surrounded by massive walls, and walled temple and private compounds suggest that reserve lines of defense may also have been prepared in advance. To judge from the effectiveness of the Akkadians in breaching and destroying walls, the arts of siege warfare were also well advanced. Presumably, these depended on the solution of the relatively simpler logistical problem of supplying armies by ship, cart, and pack train for the crucial campaigns against rebellious Sumerian cities easily accessible to the capital. Furthermore, the Mesopotamian armies were more differentiated and professional in character than seems to be implied for their Aztec counterparts by the frequent instances recounted by Spanish sources of indiscipline, disorganization, and tactical naïveté. Sumerian muster rolls and representations of battle suggest that individual units specialized in different weapons and that the employment of the phalanx was fully understood. If the leaders of such units may be likened to the Aztec nobility, their following included an at least semiprofessional nucleus of soldier-vassals bound to the palace, for which there was no Aztec equivalent. And, while it may be doubted that the lumbering four-wheel, four-equid chariots provided any substantial military advantage under most circumstances, the availability of metal in considerable quantity (on which the development of the phalanx may have depended) provided an important source of superiority in conflict with those who either did not have it or could cast it into weapons less expertly.

The possible significance of this contrast in wider social and economic terms is readily apparent. The transport of tribute from conquered towns in Mexico, depending essentially on human carriers, simultaneously provided a continuing flow of subject peoples upon whom labor services could also be imposed. Accordingly, there was little or no economic justification for large-scale dependence on slavery or permanently indentured service, and the consuming preoccupation with sacrificial cults was—if hardly "predictable"—at least not "dysfunctional."

Further, the impetus to the elite to provide leadership in agricultural management was largely absent. Their proper business on behalf of the community was war and the securing of tribute; if they succeeded in that business, agriculture would take care of itself. Only when the elite reached proportions threatening to overtax the supplies of tribute that any reasonable extension of the realm could produce (in view of the transportation problems), a condition perilously close at hand during the last years before the Conquest, did the problem of forging a managerial, investment-oriented rather than an extractive, consumption-oriented relationship to land and agriculture become an important one. It is for that reason that the activities and position of Aztec merchants are so interesting and critical. Representatives of a group that so often has been the harbinger of an atomistic, rationalizing view that in the end compels social change, the Aztec traders are reported to have begun to acquire land. Presumably they purchased it, since land was given by the king only to members of the nobility or to conspicuously successful warriors. Such purchases probably reflect upward mobility, either of individuals or of traders as a class—the acquisition of small holdings in imitation of the estates of the nobility. But it seems certain that they also reflect a dawning awareness of agriculture as a greater and more durable potential source of wealth than dependence on trade and tribute.

In Mesopotamia, on the other hand, two circumstances in particular combined to dictate an earlier and more decisive trend in the same direction: the greater functional specificity of agricultural employment from at least Protoliterate times onward and the more effectively integrated character of the larger estates on which it was practiced. The important units of production in this case were not families or communities of independently effective agriculturalists, to be shifted and recombined or put to other duties at the behest of every new owner or conquerer, but relatively large, consolidated, and complex estates. And these estates were closely tied to a particular set of landholdings by their networks of irrigation canals and groves of producing date gardens; by centrally maintained facilities for storage, agricultural equipment, and draft animals; and by the intimate symbiosis between their herds, fields, and surrounding pasture lands. Large-scale dislocation of the labor force under such conditions, whether for tributary labor service in the distant capital or for the propitiatory sacrifice, could only have jeopardized the primary resources that were the goal of conquest. And, unlike the problems of transporting bulk food stuffs to the Aztec capital (from many parts of that realm human carriers would have consumed far more than they delivered, limiting tribute from such regions to luxuries), the concentration of supplies by boat in a center like Agade could be accomplished with a comparatively minor diversion of labor. Hence in Mesopotamia it was the towns, each jealously maintaining its own local traditions and its own peasant hinterlands, that repeatedly resisted, and ultimately survived, the ebb and flow of the Akkadian conquests. It was their entrenched strength and continuity, rather than any weakness in the imperial organization of the Akkadians, that seems to account for the major differences with the realm of the Aztecs.

V

CONCLUSION

IN WHAT MUST ALWAYS BE A PROCESS OF SELECTION AND EM-phasis from among many details, valid and accurate for some purposes and not for others, the main purpose of this essay has been to suggest that two territorially extensive, complex, long-lived, innovative, characteristically "civilized" societies were *fundamentally* similar, which is not meant to imply that there is a one-for-one correspondence in all their parts—even in broadly conceived function, let alone in formal details. But the similarities are sufficiently close and numerous to suggest that in this and similar cases it is genuinely useful, that is, productive of insights at the level of understanding the individual historical sequence, to proceed at times from a generalizing, comparative stance rather than exclusively from a contrastive and compartmentalizing one.

As was indicated earlier, the course of the Urban Revolution can be described as an ascending curve taking the alternative forms of a "ramp" or a "step" (see above, p. 17). These forms are graphed in sequence A and C, respectively, in Figure 4. As an ideal type, the former perhaps implies a steady course and pace of development, a smoothly unfolding series of complementary trends following a seemingly "orthogenetic" pathway without abrupt transformations or temporary reversals. The latter emphasizes more sudden and disjunctive changes, an abrupt "step" upward to a new plateau of socio-cultural complexity, followed by oscillations above and below

170

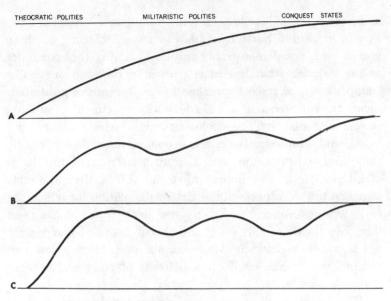

THEOCRATIC POLITIES   MILITARISTIC POLITIES   CONQUEST STATES

A

B

C

FIGURE 4. Paradigms of early urban growth

the newly elevated mean. Rather than seeking to identify long-term developmental trends and cumulative aspects of growth, it visualizes the abrupt attainment of a new, urban level as being followed only by periodic recessions without successive further advances in level until the next phase of abrupt change. Both "ramp" and "step" are intended as polar abstractions rather than empirical descriptions, of course, so paradigmatic reconstructions combining aspects of both, like that suggested by curve B, in most cases may be historically more accurate.

It should be stressed that the same paradigm is not necessarily the most fitting for all aspects of a particular historical sequence; different curves of growth may be applicable to different criteria of study. With respect to both Mesopotamia and Mexico, the "step" simile applies best if we focus on such qualities as monumentality of architecture, artistic achievement, and style. Classic Teotihuacán and Protoliterate Uruk both rise in one incredible burst to a plateau that, according to these criteria, was not demonstrably surpassed during the remainder of the sequence that has been presented for each area. The "ramp" simile, or some approximation of it, requires a different focus: the emergence of increasingly autonomous, differentiated sectors of social activity—socioeconomic classes; military, political, and administrative elites; economic networks of tribute, trade and redistribution, etc. The attractiveness of this focus of interest is, as was indicated at the outset, that it directs attention toward aspects of the Urban Revolution for which the early written evidence is directly pertinent. Hence it has been the main theme of this essay, which has assumed and sought to demonstrate that in Mesopotamia and Mexico we can identify intelligible, *cumulative* patterns of change that were strikingly similar.

Whichever focus of study, and corresponding polar paradigm, we choose to follow, it is interesting to note that approximately the same correlation of homotaxial phases seems to hold between the Mesopotamian and Mexican sequences. The rough equivalence of Teotihuacán and Protoliterate Uruk with respect to stylistic virtuosity and monumentality of architecture has already been referred to. Since both reflect an all-embracing intensity of religious styles and an apparently unquestioned ascendancy of theocratic leadership, they also serve as starting points of equivalent sequences of change along the axis of social differentiation. Moreover, the appearance of the first formally represented traces of militarism in late Protoliterate times and toward the end of Teotihuacán, as well as the bifurcation between religious and political institutions toward the end of the occupation of Tula and during the Early Dynastic period, corroborates the main lines of the correlation set forward in Figure 1 and followed throughout this essay. Finally, the very close and detailed similarities in the organization of the Akkadian and Aztec realms of extended conquest,

trade, and tribute seem to confirm the postulated equivalence
of the terminal points of our sequences.

There are differences as well as similarities in the course
of developments in the two areas, and they also can be at least
partially expressed in terms of the alternative paradigms given
in Figure 4. For Mesopotamia, the relatively smoothly rising
"ramp" of the A alternative is as close and reasonable an approximation as any other of the emergence of autonomous
sectors of social activity. In prehispanic Mexico, on the other
hand, there were more marked periods of political fragmenta-
tion, discontinuity in occupation, and decline in the crafts between the successive periods of intensified integration and
interregional contact under the aegis of centers like Teotihuacán, Tula, and Tenochtitlán. Such phases of advance and
decline during the latter part of the Urban Revolution, together
with the exceptional size already attained by Teotihuacán very
early in the sequence, argue against the simile of the "ramp."
Probably the available evidence provides no basis for deciding
whether B or C is the more plausible alternative expression
of the Mexican sequence considered as an isolate. However,
the impressive overall similarities with Mesopotamia tend to
incline the balance in favor of an intermediate alternative like
B rather than the distinctively different, "step"-like process
reconstructed in C.

There are, in short, differences as well as similarities in the
course of development followed in the two areas, and the objective of systematic comparison would not be advanced by
ignoring the former and overstressing the latter. We have dealt,
to be sure, with independently recurring examples of a single,
fundamental, cause-and-effect sequence. Each example, however, involved not the reenactment of a predetermined pattern
but a continuing interplay of complex, locally distinctive forces
whose specific forms and effects cannot be fully abstracted
from their immediate geographical and historical contexts. In
that sense, early urban societies in Mesopotamia and Mexico

were regionally specialized variants built around a common processual "core," and there are aspects of the two specializations whose essential features may still elude us. In that sense also, these are historical sequences whose determinate relationships can only be discovered or imposed retrospectively and surely were never apparent to their protagonists.

And what of the specializations themselves? How may we succinctly describe the differences between two alternative pathways leading from a common origin among village agriculturalists to a common end in urban states and primitive imperial systems? The foregoing analysis suggests that among the crucially distinctive features of early Mesopotamian civilization were its relatively more compact area and settlement pattern and correspondingly more unified culture; its prevailing ability to dissolve the ethnic identifications of immigrants and to foster urban loyalties instead; the striking continuity of occupation and tradition in all its major cultural centers; its precocious innovativeness in the crafts and hence its rapidly, cumulatively advancing technology; and its emphasis on the development of administrative and redistributive institutions concerned with economic management. In central Mexico, on the other hand, smaller, more widely dispersed valley enclaves were the characteristic units of settlement; the basic continuities were found more often in self-conscious, periodically mobile ethnic groups than in urban centers; technology remained essentially static over long periods; and there was more emphasis on market integration than on vertically organized redistributive networks.

What seems overwhelmingly most important about these differences is how small they bulk, even in aggregate, when considered against the mass of similarities in form and process. In short, the parallels in the Mesopotamian and Mexican "careers to statehood" (Gearing 1962), in the forms that institutions ultimately assumed as well as in the processes leading to them, suggest that both instances are most significantly characterized by a common core of regularly occurring features. We discover anew that social behavior conforms not merely to laws but to a limited number of such laws, which perhaps has always been taken for granted in the case of cultural subsystems (e.g., kinship) and among "primitives" (e.g., hunting bands). Not merely as an abstract article of faith but as a valid starting point for detailed, empirical analysis, it applies equally well to some of the most complex and creative of human societies.

REFERENCES CITED

ACOSTA, JORGE R.
   1956   Interpretación de algunos de los datos obtenidos
               relativos a la época Tolteca. Revista Mexicana de
               Estudios Antropológicos 14: 75–110.

ACOSTA SAIGNES, MIGUEL
   1945   Los Pochteca. Acta Anthropologica, Vol. 1, no. 1.
               Mexico, D.F.
   1946   Los Teopixque. Revista Mexicana de Estudios
               Antropológicos 8: 147–205.

ADAMS, ROBERT McC.
   1958   Survey of ancient watercourses and settlements
               in central Iraq. Sumer 14: 101–3.
   1960a   Factors influencing the rise of civilization in the
               alluvium: illustrated by Mesopotamia. In City
               invincible: an Oriental Institute symposium, ed.
               Carl H. Kraeling and Robert McC. Adams. Chi-
               cago, University of Chicago Press.
   1960b   Early civilizations, subsistence and environment.
               In City Invincible: an Oriental Institute sympo-
               sium, ed. Carl H. Kraeling and Robert McC.
               Adams. Chicago, University of Chicago Press.
   1963   The origins of agriculture. In Horizons of anthro-
               pology, ed. Sol Tax. Chicago, Aldine Publishing
               Co.
   1965   Land behind Baghdad: a history of settlement
               on the Diyala plains. Chicago, University of Chi-
               cago Press.

ARMILLAS, PEDRO
   1951   Techologia, formaciones socio-económicas y re-

ligion en Mesoamerica. *In* The civilizations of ancient America: XXIX International Congress of Americanists, Selected Papers, Vol. 1, ed. Sol Tax. Chicago, University of Chicago Press.

1964a Condiciones ambientales y movimientos de pueblos en la frontera septentrional de Mesoamerica. *In* Homenaje a Fernando Marquez-Miranda. Madrid and Seville, Universidades de Madrid y Sevilla.

1964b Northern Mesoamerica. *In* Prehistoric man in the New World, ed. Jesse D. Jennings and Edward Norbeck. Chicago, University of Chicago Press.

BARLOW, ROBERT H.

1949 The extent of the empire of the Culhua Mexica. Ibero-Americana, Vol. 28. Berkeley, University of California Press.

BARTH, FREDERIK

1961 Nomads of south Persia: the Basseri tribe of the Khamseh confederacy. Oslo, Oslo University Press.

BORAH, WOODROW, AND SHERBURNE F. COOK

1963 The aboriginal population of central Mexico on the eve of the Spanish Conquest. Ibero-Americana, Vol. 45. Berkeley, University of California Press.

BOTTÉRO, JEAN

1965 Das erste semitische Grossreich. *In* Die altorientalischen Reiche, I: Fischer Weltgeschichte, Bd. 2, ed. Elena Cassin, Jean Bottéro, and Jean Vercoutter. Frankfurt am Main, Fischer Bücherei.

BRAIDWOOD, ROBERT J., AND GORDON R. WILLEY (eds.)

1962 Courses toward urban life: archeological considerations of some cultural alternates. Viking Fund Publications in Anthropology, no. 32.

CASO, ALFONSO

1963 Land tenure among the ancient Mexicans. American Anthropologist 65: 863–78.

CHAPMAN, ANNE C.

1957 Port of trade enclaves in Aztec and Maya civilization. *In* Trade and market in the early empires, ed. Karl Polanyi, Conrad M. Arensberg, and Harry W. Pearson. Glencoe, Ill., Free Press and Falcon's Wing Press.

CHILDE, V. GORDON
1950   The urban revolution. Town Planning Review 21: 3–17.
1952   New light on the most ancient East. London, Routledge and Kegan Paul.

COOK, SHERBURNE F., AND WOODROW BORAH
1963   Quelle fut la stratification sociale au Centre du Mexique durant la première moitié du XVIᵉ siècle? Annales 18: 226–58.

CORTÉS, HERNAN
1952   Cartas de relación de la Conquista de México. Puebla, Publicaciones de la Universidad de Puebla.

DEIMEL, ANTON
1931   Sumerische Tempelwirtschaft zur Zeit Urukaginas und seiner Vorgänger. Analecta Orientalia, no. 2. Rome, Pontifical Biblical Institute.

DIAKONOFF, IGOR M.
1954   Sale of land in pre-Sargonic Sumer. *In* Papers presented by the Soviet delegation at the XXIII International Congress of Orientalists, Assyriology Section. Moscow, Publishing House of the U.S.S.R. Academy of Sciences.

DIAZ DEL CASTILLO, BERNAL
1960   Historia verdadera de la Conquista de la Nueva España. 5th ed. Mexico, D.F., Editorial Porrua.

DIBBLE, CHARLES E.
1951   Codex Xolotl. Mexico, D.F., Editorial Jus.

DURÁN, DIEGO
1867–80   Historia de las Indias de Nueva España y islas de tierra firma. 2 vols. Mexico, D.F., Impr. de J. M. Andrade y F. Escalante.

EDZARD, DIETZ O.
1965   Die frühdynastische Zeit. *In* Die altorientalischen Reiche, I: Fischer Weltgeschichte, Bd. 2, ed. Elena Cassin, Jean Bottéro, and Jean Vercoutter. Frankfurt am Main, Fischer Bücherei.

EISENSTADT, S. N.

1963   The political systems of empires. New York, Free
              Press of Glencoe.

1964   Social change, differentiation and evolution.
              American Sociological Review 29: 375–86.

FALLERS, LLOYD A.

1964   Social stratification and economic processes. In
              Economic transition in Africa, ed. Melville J.
              Herskovits and M. Harwitz. Evanston, North-
              western University Press.

FALKENSTEIN, ADAM

1954   La cité-temple sumérienne. Cahiers d'Histoire
              Mondiale 1: 784–814.

FALKENSTEIN, ADAM, AND WOLFRAM VON SODEN

1953   Sumerische und akkadische Hymnen und Gebete.
              Zurich, Artemis Verlag.

FINKELSTEIN, J. J.

1963   Mesopotamian historiography. American Philo-
              sophical Society, Proceedings 107: 461–72.

FINLEY, MOSES I.

1964   Between slavery and freedom. Comparative
              Studies in Society and History 6: 233–49.

FLANNERY, KENT V.

1965   The ecology of early food production in Meso-
              potamia. Science 147: 1247–56.

FRANKFORT, HENRI

1939   Cylinder seals. London, Macmillan.

FRIED, MORTON H.

1960   On the evolution of social stratification and the
              state. In Culture in history: essays in honor of
              Paul Radin, ed. Stanley Diamond. New York,
              Columbia University Press.

GADD, C. J.

1962   The cities of Babylonia. Cambridge Ancient His-
              tory, 2d ed., Vol. 1, chap. 13 (preprint). Cam-
              bridge, Cambridge University Press.

1963   The Dynasty of Agade and the Gutian invasion.
              Cambridge Ancient History, 2d ed., Vol. 1, chap.
              19 (preprint). Cambridge, Cambridge University
              Press.

180 *The Evolution of Urban Society*

GARELLI, PAUL (ed.)
1960   Gilgames et sa légende. Cahiers du Groupe François Thureau-Dangin, no. 1. Paris, Imp. Nationale Librairie C. Klincksieck.

GEARING, FRED
1962   Priests and warriors: social structures for Cherokee politics in the 18th century. American Anthropological Association, Memoir 93.

GEERTZ, CLIFFORD
1964   Tihingan: a Balinese village. Bijdragen 120: 1–33.

GELB, IGNACE J.
1957   Glossary of Old Akkadian. Materials for the Assyrian Dictionary, no. 3. Chicago, University of Chicago Press.
1964   Social stratification in the Old Akkadian period. In Proceedings of the XXV International Congress of Orientalists, Vol. 1. Moscow.
1965   The ancient Mesopotamian ration system. Journal of Near Eastern Studies 24: 230–43.

GIBSON, CHARLES
1964   The Aztecs under Spanish rule. Stanford, Stanford University Press.

GÜTERBOCK, HANS G.
1934   Die historische Tradition und ihre literarische Gestaltung bei Babyloniern und Hethitern bis 1200. Zeitschrift für Assyriologie 42: 1–91.

JACOBSEN. THORKILD
1939   The Sumerian Kinglist. Oriental Institute Assyriological Studies, no. 11. Chicago, University of Chicago Press.
1957   Early political developments in Mesopotamia. Zeitschrift für Assyriologie 52: 91–140.
1960   The waters of Ur. Iraq 22: 174–85.
1963   Ancient Mesopotamian religion: the central concerns. Proceedings of the American Philosophical Society 107: 473–84.

JACOBSEN, THORKILD, AND SAMUEL N. KRAMER
1953   The myth of Inanna and Bilulu. Journal of Near Eastern Studies 12: 160–88.

JIMÉNEZ MORENO, WIGBERTO
1958   Historia antigua de Mexico. 3d ed. (mimeo-
            graphed). Mexico, D.F., Escuela Nacional de
            Antropología e Historia.

KATZ, FRIEDRICH
1956   Die sozialökonomischen Verhältnisse bei den Az-
            teken im 15. und 16. Jahrhundert. Ethnograph-
            isch-Archäologische Forschungen, Bd. 3, Teil 2.
            Berlin, VEB Deutscher Verlag der Wissenschaf-
            ten.

KIRCHOFF, PAUL
1954   Land tenure in ancient Mexico. Revista Mexicana
            de Estudios Antropológicos 14: 351–62.
1955   Quetzalcoatl, Huemac, y el fin de Tula. Cuader-
            nos Americanos 14: 163–96.
1959   The principles of clanship in human society. In
            Readings in Anthropology, Vol. 2, ed. Morton H.
            Fried. New York, Thomas Y. Crowell Co.

KRAMER, SAMUEL N.
1963   The Sumerians: their history, culture, and char-
            acter. Chicago, University of Chicago Press.

KRICKEBERG, WALTER
1964   Las antiguas culturas Mexicanas. Mexico, D.F.,
            Fondo de Cultura Económica.

KROEBER, ALFRED L.
1953   The delimitation of civilizations. Journal of the
            History of Ideas 14: 264–75.

LAMBERT, MAURICE
1953   La periode PréSargonique. Sumer 9: 198–213.

LEACH, EDMUND R.
1961   Pul Eliya: a village in Ceylon. Cambridge, Cam-
            bridge University Press.

LEEMANS, W. F.
1950   The Old Babylonian merchant: his business and
            social position. Leiden, E. J. Brill.

LEÓN PORTILLA, MIGUEL
1959   The concept of the state among the ancient Az-
            tecs. Alpha Kappa Deltan 30: 7–13.

LINTON, RALPH
1939   The Tanala of Madagascar. *In* The individual
            and his society, ed. Abram Kardiner. New York,
            Columbia University Press.

MILLON, RENÉ
n.d.   Teotihuacán.

MONZÓN, ARTURO
1949   El calpulli en la organización social de los Te-
            nochca. Publicaciones del Instituto de Historia,
            no. 14. Mexico, D.F.

MORGAN, LEWIS H.
1963   Ancient society, ed. Eleanor B. Leacock. Cleve-
            land and New York, World Publishing Co., Meri-
            dian Books.

MUMFORD, LEWIS
1960   University city. *In* City invincible: an Oriental
            Institute symposium, ed. Carl H. Kraeling and
            Robert McC. Adams. Chicago, University of
            Chicago Press.

MURPHY, ROBERT F., and LEONARD KASDAN
1959   The structure of parallel cousin marriage. Amer-
            ican Anthropologist 61: 17–29.

OPPENHEIM, A. LEO
1960   Assyriology: why and how? Current Anthropol-
            ogy 1: 409–22. *Reprinted in* Oppenheim 1964.
1964   Ancient Mesopotamia: portrait of a dead civi-
            lization. Chicago, University of Chicago Press.

ORANS, MARTIN
1966   Surplus. Human Organization (in press).

PALERM, ANGEL
1954   La distribucion del regadio en el area central
            de Mesoamerica. Ciencias Sociales 5: 2–15, 64–
            74.
1956   Notas sobre las construcciones militares y la
            guerra en Mesoamerica. Anales del Instituto Na-
            cional de Antropologia y Historia 8: 123–34.

PALERM, ANGEL, AND ERIC R. WOLF
1957   Ecological potential and cultural development
            in Mesoamerica. *In* Studies in human ecology.

Panamerican Union, Social Science Monographs, no. 3.

PERROT, JEAN
1964   Civilisations préhistoriques et protohistoriques du moyen Orient: coordination des recherches. Paris, Centre National de la Recherche Scientifique.

POLANYI, KARL, CONRAD M. ARENSBERG, AND
  HARRY W. PEARSON (eds.)
1957   Trade and market in the early empires. Glencoe, Ill., Free Press and Falcon's Wing Press.

PRITCHARD, JAMES B. (ed.)
1950   Ancient Near Eastern texts relating to the Old Testament. Princeton, Princeton University Press.

RADIN, PAUL
1920   The sources and authenticity of the history of the ancient Mexicans. University of California Publications in American Archaeology and Ethnology, no. 17.

REDFIELD, ROBERT
1953   The primitive world and its transformations. Ithaca, Cornell University Press.

RUSSELL, R. J.
1958   Late ancient and medieval populations. Transactions of the American Philosophical Society, Vol. 48, no. 3.

SAHAGUN, BERNARDINO DE
1950–   Florentine Codex, General history of the things of New Spain, ed. Arthur J. O. Anderson and Charles E. Dibble. Salt Lake City, University of Utah Press.

SANDERS, WILLIAM T.
1956   The central Mexican symbiotic region: a study in prehistoric settlement patterns. In Prehistoric settlement patterns in the New World, ed. Gordon R. Willey. Viking Fund Publications in Anthropology, no. 23.
n.d.   Teotihuacán Valley Project: preliminary report, 1960–63 field seasons (mimeographed).

Schneider, Anna
    1920   Die sumerische Tempelstadt. Essen, G. D. Bäde-
                ker.

Soustelle, Jacques
    1962   The daily life of the Aztecs on the eve of the
                Spanish Conquest (tr. from the French by Pa-
                trick O'Brian). New York, Macmillan.

Steward, Julian H.
    1955   Theory of culture change. Urbana, University of
                Illinois Press.

Wittfogel, Karl A.
    1957   Oriental despotism: a comparative study of total
                power. New Haven, Yale University Press.

Wolf, Eric R.
    1959   Sons of the shaking earth. Chicago, University
                of Chicago Press.

Wolf, Eric R., and Angel Palerm
    1955   Irrigation in the old Acolhua domain. South-
                western Journal of Anthropology 11: 265–81.

Woolley, C. L.
    1934   The royal cemetery. Ur Excavations, Vol. 2.
                London and Philadelphia, published for the
                Trustees of the British Museum and the Museum
                of the University of Pennsylvania.

Zurita, Alonso de
    1941   Breve y sumaria relación de los señores y ma-
                neras y diferencias que habia de ellos en Nueva
                España. *In* Nueva colección de documentos para
                la historia de Mexico, ed. J. Garcia Icazbalceta.
                Mexico, D.F., Editorial Salvador Chávez Hayhoe.

INDEX

185